Modern Homestead
Grow, Raise, Create

FULCRUM
GOLDEN, COLORADO

RENEE WILKINSON

Library of Congress Cataloging-in-Publication Data
Wilkinson, Renee.
  Modern homestead : grow, raise, create / by Renee
Wilkinson.
     p. cm.
  Includes bibliographical references and index.
  ISBN 978-1-55591-748-7 (pbk.)
  1. Urban gardening. 2. Urban livestock production
systems. I. Title.

  SB453.W4925 2011
  640--dc22

                        2010044146

Printed in Malaysia
0 9 8 7 6 5 4 3 2 1

Design: Jack Lenzo
Cover image: Isaac Viel

Fulcrum Publishing
4690 Table Mountain Drive, Suite 100
Golden, Colorado 80403
800-992-2908 • 303-277-1623
www.fulcrumbooks.com

For Jay—
my love and gratitude
until the end of our days

CONTENTS

Acknowledgments

Thank you to Jay, my partner in all things, for answering the question "Could I write a book?" Your steadfast belief that I could pull this off fueled my determination, and your endless support pushed me further than I could have gone on my own.

Many thanks are extended to Harper Keeler and all the folks at the Urban Farm for their guidance and for providing a welcoming place for me to dig my hands into the soil. Thank you also to Susan Hill Newton at Fulcrum Publishing for asking me if I had ever thought about writing a book. I am grateful for your wisdom and calm. Isaac Viel, you can sure take some beautiful photographs.

How lucky am I to have such lovely friends as Anne Bedney, Denise Hampton, Erika Thompson, Madeline Carroll, Claudia Sims, Rebekah Milani, and Vivan Schoung. Thank you for being such real, empowering women. Laura Irwin, you kept my head from spinning with your sound and seasoned writing advice. Thank you to Patty Stevenson for sharing your community gardening wisdom, and Nate Ulrich for showing off the bees. Deck Family Farm let us come visit their animals so we could have some great pictures of furry and feathered critters.

My grandparents thought they would never see the day when chickens moved back into the city. Thank you for the years of advice and stories that turned my little garden into a thriving homestead.

And finally, thank you to the little ones, Evan, Alex, and Casey. We are trying to clean this planet up for you guys before we leave it—sorry for the mess.

Introduction

My homesteading life seemed like a new, bold venture when I first picked up a spade as an adult and stood over a barren patch of dirt. I felt nervous, excited, and determined.

My previous life as a renter included small garden experiments with herbs clustered on a windowsill or a few vegetables shoved into some tight spot in a flower bed. Every year of my renting life I moved in the summer, right at harvest season. The indoor plants moved with me, but the outside ones I had grown just in time for new renters to enjoy the fruits of my labor. I didn't realize it at the time, but I actually had a ton of grown-up experience growing vegetables—I was just never there to enjoy them.

My husband, Jay, and I had just taken possession of our first house and were feeling overwhelmed with our lack of knowledge. We didn't know the first thing about home repairs, and our lawn was already in desperate need of mowing. But despite all those worries, I found myself thinking more and more about that big empty canvas of a backyard and mentally staking out my future garden.

Around the time we bought our house, I had been reading lots of books on growing your own vegetables and keeping chickens. I wanted to live more self-sufficiently on our new plot, but I didn't know exactly what to do. I began to sketch out on paper how to transform an endless lawn into a productive, edible landscape. It's one thing to draw on paper, though, and another to actually do it. What if I tore up all the grass, put in fruit trees and shrubs, and the whole thing looked horrible? What if it all died because I didn't do it right?

At the time, I found bafflingly little information online about modern homesteading in the city. So I thought, hey, why not make my own source of information—a garden journal of sorts. This led me to start my blog: Hip Chick Digs. I figured that if the whole thing ended in a big failure, at least others could learn from my mistakes.

It turned out that there really weren't major failures. I lost a plant here and there, but for the most part the garden blossomed over the next few years into a lively space humming with bees and ladybugs, ripe with figs and veggies. Meanwhile, the blog became a connection to other urban homesteaders, with people actively commenting on my posts and sharing tips. Yet there was still a much greater resource that I had not discovered: my own homesteading heritage.

I described myself as a newbie gardener, but in fact I grew up on an urban farm. We lived in the city in an old house with a quarter acre of yard my parents devoted to a garden and an orchard. My father woke us up early on summer mornings to weed between rows of corn, harvest raspberries, and collect fallen apples. As a child I would often intentionally forget my house keys as an excuse to spend the rest of my day after school in the garden, playing and stuffing myself with sugar snap peas. My parents would return home to see I had spoiled my dinner and made little progress on my homework.

We had a cellar in the basement where I would be sent every evening before dinner to gather jars of applesauce, peaches, or pickles for dinner. My mother's time spent canning and pickling the fruit and vegetables from our urban garden seemed like a routine that must have been going on in everyone's household during the summer and fall months. Surely all of my friends had a freezer in the basement too, filled with meat purchased from the local rancher.

As an adult, I realized how lucky I was to grow up on an urban homestead. I had assumed all of my childhood memories didn't translate to actual gardening knowledge, but it turns out they did.

Standing with a spade in hand at our new house, I already knew some basics.

For example, when you water vegetables the water needs to really soak in well, not just get sprinkled on the top. I remembered how tomatoes don't like to get their leaves wet, so my dad would make little moats for the water to pool in for when they got thirsty. I knew the asparagus at our old house would get buggy sometimes, so we needed to pick the bugs off periodically. But other things like onions and potatoes seemed to just grow without us doing much work at all.

I began asking my parents questions about gardening problems and preserving. My mom dug her old canning equipment out of a box in the garage and let me use it to experiment with new recipes as well as my favorites from childhood. When there was a question she couldn't answer, she told me to call (who else?) *her* mom, Grandma Egger.

In time my grandparents became my most useful resource for anything homesteading related. This made sense, because keeping chickens and growing your own food actually skipped most of my parents' generation; it was in the last half of the twentieth century that the industrialized farming revolution booted most American households off the homesteading path. Urban gardens could be neglected because supermarkets were opening across the country, offering cheaper food choices that required less preparation time.

My conversations with my grandparents started off with vegetables and berry preserves, but got much deeper into homesteading life as time went on. I learned that I was actually a sixth generation

Oregon Trail pioneer, with my grandmother's great-grandparents completing that daunting journey back in 1851. I mentioned I was thinking about keeping some backyard chickens and waited for them to scoff, but they got excited instead.

It turns out both of my sets of grandparents kept chickens in the city. My little ninety-six-year-old nana kept about thirty hens and would sell the eggs to make an income during lean times, which was pretty much all the time since she had nine kids to feed. They were delighted with my backyard livestock ventures and eager to share advice and memories of their urban farming days. Meanwhile, I was reading newspaper articles about backyard chickens, reporting them in a breathless tone like it was a breaking news story! It was funny, and at the same time a little sad as I realized how totally disconnected modern America is from its roots.

All in all, sharing knowledge about simple living, growing your own food, raising backyard livestock, and preserving the harvest brought me much closer to my family. We have something exciting to talk about every time we get together. My grandpa Egger gave me his old books on composting, and my grandma Egger still sends me home from visits with armfuls of produce to preserve.

As my gardening savvy increased, so did my desire to learn more about the history of homesteading. I read diaries from early homesteaders, looked at records of what items people packed for the journey west, and began to fill in a lot of details for myself about what life was like for them.

Life was hard for those early homesteaders. The Homestead Act of 1862 allowed citizens to claim 160 acres, or a quarter of a square mile, of land out West. If they managed to stay alive for five years, the land became theirs outright. Can you imagine loading up your entire family and heading thousands of miles into the unknown? The dispatches that came back East were full of frightening tales of rugged terrain, imposing mountains, and wild rivers. I stopped worrying so much about whether my tomatoes were planted in the perfect place.

Coming from the eastern cities, many early homesteaders had no farming background—they were complete newbies. This is when I started to realize that a return to homesteading life was not such a leap for us modern folks. Before setting out on dusty trails, the early homesteaders bought guidebooks that offered advice on routes, supplies to pack, and potential threats along the trail. Once they staked their claim, they relied on how-to-garden pamphlets and put their meager knowledge to work.

They, too, had failures along the way to getting established on the frontier. Crops were planted too early or too late, livestock was lost to death or injury, and the weather threw them curveballs. But they learned from their mistakes and were courageous (and hungry) enough to keep trying. They relied heavily on the advice and help of seasoned neighbors, and thus community became a very important aspect of life, as everyone needed to be able to count on each other. Each season it became just a little bit easier to keep those cupboards full for the coming winter.

So it turns out they were not so different from you and me. Like those trailblazers, maybe you, too, have never put a seed in the ground or known what it feels like to hold a still-warm, freshly hatched egg in your hands. And you, too, will undoubtedly have failures along the bumpy ride of homesteading. You share their gritty determination to live a more self-sufficient life and to deepen your connection to the land. Perhaps your motivation is not simply the lure of the wild and untamed West, but rather a desire to cultivate a more sustainable future.

In this book, I share generations of homesteading wisdom to help bring modern generations back to the land. There are projects and tips here that anyone can use, whether your homestead is a studio apartment or a sprawling yard in the suburbs. You can take comfort in knowing our ancestors probably had less knowledge than you have today, yet they created parcels of land that flourished under the harshest of circumstances.

Together we can reclaim that pioneering spirit. Be brave, go forth, dig in!

Chapter One
STAKE YOUR CLAIM

No matter where you live, you can transform your home into a modern homestead. Gardens can sprout up on windowsills or in raised vegetable beds. Patios can welcome mini–chicken coops, and backyards can be home to a couple milk goats. Cupboard shelves can fill with collections of homemade sauces and jars of dried herbs. Just like it was for the early pioneers before us, it's all about taking a good look around our plots of land to decide how to best go forth.

This chapter is designed to walk you through the process of determining what projects will be easiest for you to create. Maybe your ultimate goal is to live on a totally self-sufficient homestead in the next ten years—good for you! But you don't need to wait ten years to start making that transition. You can make it today, even in the smallest of spaces.

Renting Your Homestead

You do not need to own your space to have an urban homestead—renters can be homesteaders too. It's easy to create a spread that can move with you a year, two years, or five years down the road. Vegetables can be grown in containers, birdhouses can come down off hooks, and canned goodies can be packed up and moved with everything else.

The one major force that needs to be reckoned with before you determine which projects to tackle is the dreaded *L* word: the landlord. You don't need to consult the landlord about making homemade cleaners or whether you grow lettuce in a hanging basket on your balcony. But you will need to consult the landlord about anything related to feathered or furry residents and anything that requires drilling into the walls.

As renters, we begin to learn that where we live is about more than just location, how cute the space is, and how it is priced. It's also about renting from an easy-to-work-with landlord who will be flexible about your green-living ideas—which means you may rent from them longer term. If your landlord is not okay with you keeping some bantam chickens on the balcony or patio, put that idea on hold and invest your energy in other projects. If your landlord is so uptight that he or she will absolutely not allow a window

box to be drilled into the exterior wall, consider using one that hangs off the window ledge instead.

I do not recommend making things uncomfortable or hostile by going against the rules your landlord has laid out for you when you agreed to rent from him. Challenge yourself to make an urban homestead in any situation, and be more selective about whom to rent from next time around. When it comes time for your lease to be up, look for a great rental that also comes with a good landlord who respects your lifestyle choices and wants you to be happy where you live by making it your home. They are out there and, depending on where you live, they might not be so hard to find. Broaden your rental search to posting boards at natural grocery stores that include houses and apartments for rent—the landlords of these places might be more receptive to urban homestead activities.

Small Spaces

My very first garden was in a downtown apartment building with no outdoor space. Instead, I had east-facing windows, some of which were shaded by trees. The shadier window ledges were for houseplants and alfalfa sprouts, while the sunnier ledges held a collection of small herb pots. I had fresh chives for baked potatoes, basil for pasta, and sprouts for sandwiches. It was a modest but respectable start in a very limited space, and every garden after grew in size.

In small spaces, the first place to consider making changes is behind the cupboard doors. Here in the dark and quiet are the canned foods, dried culinary herbs, and household cleaners we use all the time. You can spend less time and money at the grocery store by making these products yourself using higher-quality ingredients that are better for the planet.

Think about hosting an annual holiday craft party where guests can make natural bath salts or hand salves to give away as gifts. Chapter four gives you fun recipes that are easy to prepare and require just a few ingredients. You and your friends can collectively buy the supplies, and everyone splits the cost. You won't end up storing large quantities of raw materials in your limited cabinet space, because the ingredients are simple and everyone takes their share at the end of the party.

On that same theme, preserving food through canning and drying may not be feasible, since you will likely need equipment that you then have to store most of the year. Instead, focus on buying produce in bulk from either the farmers' market or local farms directly to take home and freeze. This is an opportunity to support the sustainable farming industry in your area.

Tomatoes bought in bulk from the local farmers' market.

Maybe you only have a freezer big enough for a couple bags here and there, so plan on preserving your two favorite things. Frozen corn can magically bring back the memories of summer when made into chowder in the winter months. Make sure to leave a little room for a bag or two of berries picked from a local farm to jazz up Sunday-morning pancakes. Chapter four covers the basics on different food preservation methods, including recipes for you to use now or at your next spread.

Now it's time to take a look at any sunny spots around your space. Is there a windowsill where you can cultivate a small herb garden? If sunny space is hard to find, several perennial herbs still do well in the shade. A little patio or front porch can be the perfect spot for a small collection of pots or a larger container of mixed herbs. Think about making a little room between perennials for some basil and cilantro plants, which are annuals. You can preserve what you grow by freezing small batches of pesto and drying herb bouquets. Once you have dried a variety of herbs, come up with your own herb blend to keep in the spice rack or use my Aunt Emily's recipe on page 178.

A mesclun mix of lettuces does not need very much space to grow, and lettuce is a cut-and-come-again crop, meaning it keeps growing as you use it. A hanging basket can easily be filled with a

Herb garden hanging outside the kitchen window.

mixture of greens and hung right outside your window. Just snip them as needed for salads all season. Chapter two shows you how to plant and care for your hanging basket and gives you even more ideas for growing edibles in tight spots.

Indoor houseplants really make a place feel like home. They are beautiful to look at, and they help keep our air clean. Instead of the regular run-of-the-mill houseplant, make a small investment in a dwarf citrus tree. Place it near a sunny window and water regularly. The plant will reward you with lush foliage, fragrant blossoms, and juicy fruit once a year. Meyer lemons, kumquats, and limes are all great choices for growing indoors.

Kumquat tree growing near a sunny window.

You can reduce your household waste and keep the garden cycle churning by making your own compost, even in an apartment. The best way to do this in tight quarters is with a small worm bin, or vermicompost system. The worm bin on page 43 can be tucked into a number of out-of-the-way places, although placing it under the kitchen sink is often the most convenient. As the food waste breaks down into nutrient-rich compost, add it to your houseplants and vegetable garden as needed.

If you have a small balcony or patio, combine your vermicompost system with a small flock of chickens. The mini–chicken coop in chapter three comfortably houses three bantam chickens. The design features a worm bin box that sits on top of the run. It's a space-saving design that does double duty.

Rooftops in densely urban areas can be a great space for honeybees to call home. The hives take up very little floor space, and the bees will happily fly through the neighborhood, pollinating trees and flowers. If you are renting, not every landlord is going to be cool about these new residents. Talk to your landlord first to see what he is open to and go from there.

If you get stuck with a "No!" kind of landlord, you can still have city critters in the way of native wildlife. Invite your pals over for a birdhouse-making party using found materials and unique decor. Hang one outside your window for little finches to raise a family in. An overwintering bee box allows native bees to hole up

somewhere safe during the cold months. Watch closely in the spring as the holes open up and baby bees emerge into the flowering world.

Being limited on space or sunlight is a great excuse to dig into a local community garden plot. There you can meet other like-minded, friendly people who are just as excited as you are about living this lifestyle of growing. Building a community of urban homesteaders allows you to share ideas back and forth and maybe even make a few new friends.

BREATHING ROOM

A home with a little elbow room expands your homesteading options even further. Your space might be a condo with a patio, a townhouse with a postage-stamp yard, or a house with a decent-sized backyard.

You have even more options to choose from—some that can be permanent and some that can remain mobile.

Having just enough space outside that gets good sunlight means you can dig deeper into the rockin' world of container vegetable gardening. Chapter two shows you what containers to use, how to get great soil, and what vegetable combinations to plant. You'll learn how to pull together several mismatched containers and make them into a stylish collection. If you have outdoor space to spare, you will learn how dwarf fruit trees and berry bushes can transform your plot into an edible estate. And knowing the basics on composting will help your homestead thrive every season.

Planting a couple wine barrel containers with vegetables can make nearly all the ingredients for a meal. An Asian-themed container garden gives you lots of possibilities for delicious stir-fry dinners, while an Italian-themed planter provides nearly all the fixings for fabulous pasta primavera. If you are renting, place the heavy wine barrels on rollers so they can roll with you on moving day. Whether you are planting in the ground or in containers, planting complete meals can ease you into cooking fresh. See just what goes where in the planting plans in chapter two.

Make a little room on the balcony or patio for a small table and a couple chairs. Having a garden means you get to enjoy the harvest, but take time to enjoy the space too. A comfortable place to sit means you can be enticed into the green space more often, with plenty of opportunities to admire your beloved plant friends and protect them from harm. Look hard around your outdoor spaces now, before you even pick up a spade, to see what you can squeeze into each nook and cranny. The smallest space can become an outdoor retreat.

You may not own a mansion, but you likely have more room for some serious food preservation. My favorite accompaniment to a leisurely morning on my container-filled patio is a thick slice of crusty toast smothered with homemade berry preserves. Trust me, you can never have too many jars in your cupboards. It might be high time you jumped on the canning bandwagon and stocked your shelves. The Forest Berry Preserves on page 172 are

Small spaces can be productive retreats.

easy to make and incredibly versatile— use on toast, muffins, as cupcake topping, or cake filling. Your kitchen may be large enough to invite some friends over for a canning party. This is a great way to catch up with each other and take home some delicious treats.

A backyard is ample room for feathered fowl like chickens and ducks. The chicken coop on page 93–95 can house three standard hens and includes storage space for all your poultry supplies. Start a

compost pile by mixing the used chicken bedding with kitchen scraps for even richer finished compost. You can look forward to brunch on the patio eating eggs from the girls and enjoying veggies straight from the garden.

SPRAWLING SPREAD

A substantial space opens up a seemingly endless array of self-sufficient possibilities. Not only can you grace your outdoor seating area with lush vegetable containers, but you can probably section off an entire portion of your backyard for a garden oasis. Find the best situation for sunlight and access to the garden hose to stake out some large raised beds.

With several raised beds to plant your crops in, spend your winter months planning a good crop-rotation schedule. Pick one or two beds to devote just to tomatoes so you can do small batch canning all summer. Dig in an orchard of pear and apple trees surrounding the raised beds to provide enough fruit for homemade chutney, like the one in chapter four.

The leaves from the fruit trees should give you enough compost material to embark on the three-bin system. This ever-producing amount of compost will boost the health and production of your urban farm.

A couple dwarf milk goats will fit cozily into a corner of the backyard, enriching that compost even further. Your homestead will be producing homegrown goodies all year, like fresh milk and herbed goat cheese. The curious goats might enjoy a free-ranging flock of ducks to share the outdoor space with too.

With milk and eggs in the refrigerator, stock up the cupboards and freezer

A chicken coop and container garden create a cozy garden space.

Raised garden beds growing purple kale, rainbow chard, and scarlet beets.

Everyone, Everywhere

The following is a collection of sustainable living practices we should all look into doing—regardless of where we live. These may seem like generally easy ideas on paper, but old habits die hard:

Eat Local
- Reduces our reliance on fossil fuels, which in turn reduces climate change
- Supports local farmers and the local economy
- Reduces dependence on industrialized food companies that use harmful chemicals on the land and in the food
- Tastes better because it was picked at prime ripeness

BYOB

- Americans use an estimated 100 billion plastic bags every year
- Plastic bags can only be recycled a few times before they head for the landfill
- Disposable bags waste energy during production and shipping to retailers
- Keep reusable bags in the car at all times, so you never forget to bring them
- Choose locally made bags even over organic, which could be sourced overseas
- Get creative by sewing up an old skirt or pillowcase and add straps to the top

Use Alternative Transportation

- Reduce your dependence on fossil fuels by using gas wisely
- Save money at the gym by walking or biking to work or to the store
- Combine trips for efficiency when you need to drive
- Use the money you save on gas to buy a morning coffee for the bus ride or better raingear for bike riding
- Donate cash savings from gas and parking costs to your favorite charity

Reduce, Reuse, Recycle
- Rebel against consumerism by living more simply, without the latest electronics or newest designer jeans
- If it's not broken, don't replace it
- If it is broken, look into repairing it before buying new
- Buy only enough groceries for the next week, to reduce wasted food
- Buy nonperishables in bulk to reduce packaging and shipping costs
- Shampoo every two to three days for healthier hair and less wasted water
- Use a water-efficient toilet, or place a filled half-gallon jug in the toilet tank so less water is flushed away
- Repurpose old clothing by sewing reusable shopping bags from them or cutting them into strips for cleaning rags (no more paper towels!)
- Check rebuilding centers for salvage items for home improvement projects
- Recycle everything you can and work on getting curbside recycling in your area if it's not there already

Trade tips and gardening woes with other hip homesteaders.

with even more harvested produce. A chest freezer in the garage can fit dozens of bags of frozen peas, beans, carrots, onions, and fruit ready for pies. Get ready to spend less time in the grocery store aisle and more time enjoying the fruits of your labor all year.

Vegetables, fruit, eggs, milk, and a continuous supply of nutrient-rich soil all being produced from your own backyard? This is the modern homesteader's dream come true!

CULTIVATE A COMMUNITY

Homesteading has never been a solitary venture—not back on the frontier and not here today. There is the neighbor who lets you know when a missing chicken turns up in her yard. Friends take turns goat-sitting for each other or doing milk duty when someone is sick with the flu. We offer to water each other's gardens while someone is away on vacation. Your local farmer mentions he is getting a bumper crop of tomatoes and offers to sell you the best lot for a discounted price. And so on and so forth. A successful homestead builds and strengthens the larger community around it.

This is where our smaller changes can often lead to bigger ones.

Garden Clubs for Nongrays

You may have a tough time finding a rockin' gardening club if you have very few to no gray hairs on your head. The topics and speakers at existing garden clubs may discuss conservation issues, native plants, and habitat, but for the most part they lack younger, energetic gardeners doing nontraditional gardening.

Do not despair! Where there is no community, you can create your own. Dig a little deeper, and you might be surprised to find an emerging community online. Talk with friends who are into urban gardening that focuses on low-cost, hip, and quirky designs and food production. Organize a reoccurring meeting time that will work for most people, like the first Saturday afternoon of the month. Decide whether the club will meet at the same place each week or rotate to different locations. Your club can meet at a local coffeehouse, plant store, park, or even in your own backyard.

Next, start building the club membership to get more like-minded folks on board. The more people you have in the club sharing ideas, offering advice, and pitching in to line up interesting speakers, the less pressure on any one person to keep the group going. Ask your local plant store if you can post a flyer about the first meeting, post the meeting information online, and ask your friends to each bring a friend.

Name your garden club! This may sound trivial, but a name can mean so much. You can attract fellow growers by taking this little step to describe your garden club in a very cool and new way. Portland Garden Club, for example, sounds pretty blah. But Punk Rock Portland Gardeners sounds a lot more entertaining, and you begin to get a mental picture of the kind of people who might belong to this club.

Hosting an annual seed swap is a great way to experiment with new, interesting vegetable varieties. It also ensures seeds get used up before they get too old and germination rates decline. Bring seed catalogs to the event and organize group orders among the members so everyone can save on shipping costs.

A tool exchange can be an interesting idea, although it requires a bit of organization and trust among members. No one, for example, needs to own their own posthole digger. If one person in the club has one already, put it on the list of tools available for trade or borrowing. Make sure the tools have a name clearly printed on them and set a time limit for borrowing, like a week at a time.

Every year the garden club could organize a bulk soil order, with members determining how much soil or soil amendments they want to add to their plots. Everyone can pay their portion of the cost, but chances are the price will be lower because you took advantage of bulk discounts. Determine which house will be the drop-off location, and have each member pick up her share over the course of a weekend.

Consider creating your own community garden if your garden club is active and motivated enough. The American Community Gardening Association can be a great resource, advising you on how the process works. It could create a very enriching community to have organized speakers and demonstrations done right there at the community garden plots. You may even be successful enough to incorporate a weekly market stand that sells excess produce to cover water and tool costs for the members.

An annual seed swap kicks off the first garden club meeting of the year.

Volunteer

Whether working as a group or as an individual, volunteering can make such a positive impact (and make you feel great too). As a society, we do too little of this these days, and there are tons of really great people out there who are looking for help. Even if you are a newbie, there is someone who would love a helping hand.

Do what your schedule allows and don't get burned out. Pick one organization to start with and allocate a couple hours a week or even a month to volunteer with them. Choose an organization that you are the most passionate about.

There are a growing number of local organizations that install vegetable gardens for low-income residents. This could be purely labor volunteering, turning over a patch of unused soil to make room for a garden. Or, you could serve as a garden mentor who checks back weekly with one family to help them learn how to grow their own food, if you have a bit more experience.

More and more local schools are finding that children's gardens teach students about the science of plants and insects, foster healthy eating habits, and encourage exercise and outdoor recreation. They offer kids a rare opportunity to connect with nature.

Some communities have a large nonprofit organization that manages the school gardens for an entire school district or county. In other communities it may be up to the individual school to create and maintain a garden. This might be done by an energetic teacher or a parent dedicated to a long-term investment in a particular school.

Volunteering for a school garden could mean a weekly commitment of coming by to help students water or plant vegetables. It could be a seasonal commitment of donating vegetables you started from seed over the winter. Or perhaps it is an every-once-in-a-while project, like helping kids build a chicken coop or some new raised beds.

Children are sponges, desperate to absorb new, fascinating discoveries. Their awe of watching a tiny pea seed sprout up into a little plant is infectious. We

Teaching children to garden encourages a lifelong love of nature.

share their same fascination—it's just more subdued. These are highly formative years in their lives. Spending a sunny afternoon watering lettuce may just change the way they look at salad forever.

In a nation that faces an obesity epidemic that has spread to our children, it is increasingly important that someone reaches out to show them where good food comes from. Even kids who say they don't like vegetables can still be tempted to try a juicy tomato they helped to grow or shell peas that they trellised. Their participation can motivate parents to learn how to cook with seasonal food and be a little more conscious about what they set out on the dinner table.

Most farmers' markets are nonprofit organizations that can always use a hand taking down or setting up tents. They can offer a great opportunity to get to know your neighbors better and make some new connections with local farms.

Many markets include an area for musicians to play or gardening experts to host demonstrations. Becoming more involved with your local market may allow you the opportunity to give input into who comes to perform or what topics experts will cover. Perhaps your local market can offer weekly cooking demonstrations from residents showcasing their favorite homemade ethnic dishes.

Getting to know your local farmers

better may open some new doors for you both. Perhaps the local honey farmer could be talked into hosting a seminar for the beginning beekeeper. The beef rancher may let you know when she is expecting to have a sale on large orders of steaks or partial orders of cows. And who better to ask advice on which variety of tomato to plant than the farmer who always sells the tastiest varieties? Hanging around the market at the end of the day to take down tents has its own set of special rewards: the day is done and the prices on unsold inventory may become just a little more negotiable.

Some of the most experienced and seasoned gardeners can be found in an often overlooked place: independent living centers/retirement homes. The elderly have a lifetime of stories and advice to share but too frequently no one to share them with. They may also be the least likely to be surprised by the idea of you keeping a flock of chickens in your urban backyard. If they didn't personally keep their own flock at one time, chances are their neighbor did.

Many of these senior centers include community garden plots that are rented out to residents. Consider contacting a senior center close to you that may need seasonal help keeping the grounds up or assisting residents with their own bed maintenance. You will learn some new tips on getting the best produce while giving someone much-needed company.

The opportunities to give back to the community through volunteer work are endless. A homestead is part of a much larger community, so let's do our part to give back to those in need. Don't run out and overcommit yourself. Just pick one or two places where you can make a difference and stick to it. It makes you feel good, and it helps the whole community grow and prosper.

Garden Tours

Most cities have some sort of annual fancy garden tour where you can see perfectly manicured ornamental yards. A few are now organizing eco-friendly garden tours, which can be a great place to get ideas on rainwater harvesting and native plantings. But perhaps the most useful place to find ideas is in the backyards of other urban homesteaders.

Sometimes the best places to get ideas for the garden can be right over the fence, at the neighbor's house. They are dealing with a similar-sized homestead and the same microclimate issues. Pull the neighborhood together for a garden-tour day if you are surrounded by an active gardening community. Print off signs and recruit participants. Then put signs in their yards on the tour day, and locals can wander out back to see what the Joneses are doing.

If you belong to a garden club, maybe each member can have a backyard open house over the spring, summer, and fall. You can see firsthand how they lay out the garden space, what composting methods they use, and what animals they keep for food production.

Cities like Portland and Denver have started annual chicken coop tours. Portland's Tour de Coops has been going on for more than seven years and is a great opportunity to reach out to locals interested in keeping a backyard flock. Participants can show off a wonderful array of creative coop designs, answer questions about keeping urban chickens, and perhaps give some people their first up-close glimpse of feathered friends.

The same idea could be applied to urbanites keeping ducks, bees, and goats. Propose the idea on your favorite Listserv or post a flyer at the feed store asking for participants. Then contact the local paper to see if they would be interested in writing a story about it. The more visible the urban homesteading effort becomes, the more people will be working toward a greener lifestyle.

Homestead Work Parties

Maintaining an urban homestead can be a rewarding activity, but the larger your plans, the more overwhelming things can get. Tackling new building projects can take much longer than anticipated, and sometimes we just need more hands working together to get something done. Band together with other growers to create work parties that take the pressure off these larger projects.

Make quick work of weeding with the help of gardening pals.

A work party should be arranged on a weekend day, when most people are typically available to help out. Perhaps every month it rotates to a new homesteader's property so everyone gets his or her turn to be the recipient of helping hands.

Be clear about what the day's work will entail, arrange carpools, and set a start and end time for the party. The recipient of the work party should be prepared with all the tools and materials needed to complete the project. It also works out well for the host to have a big, hot meal ready to serve at quitting time. Dust off the slow cooker so the meal cooks while you guys work up a sweat.

Work parties like these can really save money on labor costs. And for some reason, weeding a friend's yard is always more fun than weeding your own.

Transform an alley of weeds into a community flower bed.

Urban Beautification

There is almost always a nearby corner, alley, vacant lot, or parking strip that is a neighborhood eyesore. It has been ignored and abandoned, but you are forced to live within viewing distance of it. Give these neglected spaces a facelift by forming an urban beautification crew with neighbors and friends. Be sure to do your research first, to make sure what options you have when updating the space. You might get your do-good hand slapped for trespassing or violating some law or ordinance.

Once you get the green light, typically the first step is to simply remove trash and debris from these areas. Use caution when doing so, as all kinds of disgusting and possibly hazardous surprises could be lurking there. Wear thick leather gloves to protect yourself from broken glass or other debris. Try to salvage unusual odds and ends that could be re-created as some sort of garden art in the space. That would make an interesting statement about the value of something thrown away.

Think about posting a small sign letting other neighbors know that this area is no longer a dump site, but rather it is being reclaimed. That may encourage others to pull a weed here and there, or people may still use it as a toilet. You won't know unless you try.

It can be a really challenging feat to develop a green space on little or no budget. Work with friends to propagate

Work off brunch with friends by tending the neighborhood eyesore.

Instead, talk with your local plant shop about plants that are native to your area or ones that are extremely hardy. Regroup with friends once a week after brunch, or encourage neighbors to check on the spot on Sunday mornings to do small maintenance. Consider just starting with one small corner of the space and work on getting plants established there. If you walk to work, get into the habit of carrying a water bottle with you and stroll by the spot to water the new plants until they get established.

Your urban beautification crew can even focus on rehabilitating neglected edibles. There are lots of neglected old apple and pear trees out there in lonely alleyways. Write down where you stumble upon them and plan to go back in winter while they are dormant to prune them for fruit production. Again, be sure you are not in violation or trespassing. You could donate the produce to a local homeless shelter or make up a batch of hard cider, which doesn't necessarily require the world's best-tasting fruit.

cuttings from garden plants. In the fall, separate hardy perennials and plant half of them in the abandoned area. Even simple herbs like thyme and oregano can enhance a corner with fragrance and evergreen foliage.

It is best to avoid planting edibles in these spaces. When a space is seen as public land, it can often make passersby feel free to help themselves to anything growing there—after all, it's not technically yours, despite your goodwill and efforts. You most likely won't reap much food you sow, and plants might get damaged as others try to snag some of the bounty. Plus you can't control what might be tossed or sprayed on the space.

Nerd Nights

Find ways to arrange plant-related social gatherings to give friends a chance to hang out and learn about their favorite subject at the same time. A wine-and-plants party can be a fun way to make this happen. Ask everyone to bring over a bottle of wine and a few cuttings from their favorite plant. Spend the evening educating each other about why this plant rocks and propagate the cuttings together.

Instead of the traditional art gallery walk, talk to your local plant store about hosting a plant walk at their store. Plan for the small, informal event to happen on a Friday night and ask each friend to bring either a beverage or finger food to share. Ask the plant store to select about ten interesting and perhaps not well-known plants they can showcase. They can lead the group around that evening and talk about the individual plant's growing requirements and design uses. Or perhaps the theme is a container party, where friends arrive and the plant expert helps them select a container and planting design.

Rework the idea of a winery tour by taking a local plant nursery tour. This can be done at small, independent plant stores in the city or it could be made into a small day trip on the outskirts of town to tree and shrub nurseries. It can be a good way to get to know what different nurseries specialize in and what their plants look like once fully grown.

Chapter Two
GROW YOUR OWN

Homegrown heirloom tomatoes.

Dig In

My gardening knowledge has grown with the size of my living spaces, but it was not always easy. The windowsill of herbs at my first apartment came with me to the next one, but in addition I then had a balcony to experiment on. I brought home a habañero pepper, a cherry tomato, and some lettuce starts in containers a few days before a big vacation. I returned from my trip in the heat of summer to find my drought-tolerant herbs hanging on for dear life and my new vegetables dead as doorknobs. It felt like a big failure at the time, but I was only midway through the season. I swallowed my pride, bought some new starts, and kept them better watered. Lesson learned.

You may also lose a few plants in your first few gardens, but you will walk away from that first season with at least a few fruits from your labors. Every year you will become more seasoned and the garden more prolific. That is part of the allure of the whole thing—we can never dominate nature, we can only hope to work with her enough to learn some valuable lessons and enjoy the delicious taste of success.

The more baskets we fill with home-grown produce, the more addicted we get to growing our own food and the stronger our motivation becomes for tending the garden. But don't let your motivation get the better of you by planting more than you can reasonably tend. Always start small at the beginning, then grow the garden each season. Whether you are totally green or a well-versed gardener, set yourself up for some easy-to-grow beginner plants and throw in a few challenges to keep it interesting. Your garden should be a responsibility you find fulfillment in, not an overwhelming burden.

CREATING A GARDEN SPACE

A great garden begins with a great location. Take a good, careful look around your space to determine the best spot for

Peas save garden space by growing vertically.

your garden. The top priorities are access to sunlight, followed by soil quality, and finally convenience to things like water and tools.

Most vegetables require a minimum of six hours of direct sunlight a day. If you are not sure which places get the most sunlight, place a piece of paper and pencil near the windows that look out on your yard, patio, fire escape, or other outdoor nooks and crannies. Over the course of a week, try to record when you see sunlight versus shade.

Your notes will help you determine that one spot is sunny in the morning, but not the afternoon. Another area may not get direct sunlight at all, which tells you a shade-loving herb garden may do okay, but growing vegetables may not be great there. Eventually, you can piece together the sun patterns and find the best possibilities for your future garden.

Modern homesteads will often not have a nice, flat, open piece of land to plop a garden down into. In fact, most gardens have a mix of sunny and shady areas. If your outdoor space is heavily shaded, look for smaller pockets of sunlight. Window boxes and hanging baskets can be clustered around the sunniest sides of your apartment, with shady areas left for ornamentals. Several smaller vegetable beds can be placed in each little sunny spot in your backyard—it doesn't need to be one large continuous area.

Consider existing flower beds you may already have at your disposal. Flowers and vegetables can happily intermingle in these corners. Flowers can be planted

Sexy lettuce, pretty enough for the front yard.

to attract beneficial insects such as ladybugs, which will eat vegetables pests like aphids. The colors and textures can complement or contrast with each other to add visual appeal. Think about the thick green leaves of tulips growing up next to the dark, curling leaves of a purple kale plant. Tomatoes and brightly colored chard can add a lot of vibrancy growing in front of a dark evergreen hedge. Perhaps the entrance to your apartment building can be home to some pretty herbs in addition to ornamental shrubs.

If you are lucky enough to have a nice sunny spot for the garden patch, think in

Make sure garden spots are wheelbarrow accessible.

be so perfect if it's hidden from view and rarely visited. Think about whether you can see it through a window inside the house where you can easily notice that the lettuce needs some water. Or perhaps you pass the garden while entering or exiting the house, making it that much easier to spot slugs enjoying the all-you-can-eat salad bar. Positioning the garden within sight or along a frequented pathway ensures you will take note of problems before they become disasters.

RIP Lawns

Grassy lawns tend to suck up valuable resources and are often underused outdoor spaces. Nonetheless they are traditional and beloved, even if not well-used. Traditional grass lawns demand significant amounts of water, labor (picking weeds, mowing), and fertilizers, often the toxic varieties that slowly seep through the soil and back into our water systems. It's time to rethink that green blanket outside the house.

terms of gardening convenience. Is this spot close to the water hose? Watering will be an easier chore if the water source is close by. Can you get clunky tools like a wheelbarrow into the area if you need to add soil? Will the compost bin be close enough to haul debris to easily at the end of the season?

Out of sight, out of mind holds true in gardening. Important location considerations are accessibility and visibility. That perfect patch of unused ground your landlord said you could use on the other side of your apartment complex won't actually

Some cities in drier states, like Nevada, are outlawing lawns altogether. The local municipalities are recognizing in growing numbers what a water and resource drain a green lawn can be in arid areas. Instead they are pushing locals to plant drought-tolerant native plants. It really isn't that hair brained of an idea after all to turn over the grass carpet for smarter, harder working plantings.

Converting lawn to a vegetable garden does not mean you need to till the whole thing under. Instead, start small by converting a portion of the lawn space into garden space. Establish the edges of the garden with stones, bricks, a woven twig fence, railroad ties, or some other creative divider that will act as a visual barrier between the lawn and your new plot. You may find you don't miss the lawn that much and decide to enlarge the garden next year.

Containers

Planting containers can be made from many different types of materials, so you don't need to limit yourself to buying fancy ones from the nursery. It takes creativity, time, and legwork on your part, though, to scout out inventive containers. But the end result of a quirky garden can be worth it to those motivated to create one.

If you have the money to invest in pricey containers, by all means go for it. You will be able to get the instant gratification of an overnight container garden. Think in advance about what materials you want the containers to be made from, and shop around to get the best deals.

As you begin to assemble pots for a container garden, bigger is usually better. Small pots dry out fast and restrict plant growth. They can be okay for the little herb garden on the windowsill, but avoid small containers for thirsty vegetables.

All containers need to have at least one drainage hole at the bottom. For materials made out of metal and wood, which are more prone to rot, rust, or decay over time, make multiple drainage holes in the bottom to keep them around longer.

Ultimately your garden is your space and should reflect your own personality

Thrift-store finds create an eclectic container garden.

and style. You can try to collect pots that are all made from the same material, like all metal, for example, but mix their sizes and shapes. You may also decide to get containers made from a variety of materials but then paint them all the same color to unify the appearance. Paint metal tins to match the glazed ceramics and leave a few natural wood containers in there just to mix it up. Or decide to leave it a completely random, eclectic array! There is no right way, just your way.

My style is to combine traditional containers collected from estate sales and thrift stores with unusual, not-meant-to-be planters. One of my favorite combos starts with an assortment of large ceramic planters in various glaze colors. I then repurpose vintage out-of-commission kitchen gadgets (often thrift-store finds). I have used an old standing mixer, a blue canner with white speckles, a white metal washtub, and a blender, to name a few. I find a way to get holes in the bottom for drainage and am left with a very quirky, entertaining container garden.

Traditional containers are mixed with old metal stockpots.

As you seek out containers, here are some pros and cons of the different pot materials to choose from:

- Ceramic—Clay is very porous and when left unglazed, plants dry out very quickly from the sides. Glazed pots, however, are better at holding in water and often very attractive. Ceramic pots would be your heaviest and most expensive option. Think about placing large pots on stands that you can wheel around when needed.

- Wood—Eventually any planter made of wood will deteriorate, but you may have several garden seasons ahead before that happens. They can have a rustic elegance to them as they age, and I enjoy how they show some garden memory from one season to the next. Wood containers can also be sourced around town for free. Think about using fruit crates, wine boxes, old toy chests, dresser drawers, and more. Painting or sealing the wood will help it last longer, but be careful to use a nontoxic option. Avoid treated cedar, which has been processed with chemicals that can make their way onto your dinner plate.

- Plastic—Although not always the most durable or attractive, plastic containers are going to be the cheapest and lightest option. Their looks are improving as modern designers create brightly colored, interestingly shaped pots. You can find tons of abandoned containers at garage sales, thrift stores, and rummage sales. I have reused large black plastic containers from nursery trees, so they were essentially free. These big ones are often thicker and last longer. They are also large enough so you can plant several different types of veggies in one pot. Several options are emerging that use 100 percent recycled plastic.

Metal—There may be some eventual rust with metal containers, but that can add interesting character to your container garden. Add extra drainage holes at the bottom to give them the longest life. You can buy large containers used as ice buckets, or you can reuse empty coffee cans and tins. Metal is also easy to paint if you are trying to match colors.

Plant-derived containers—Relatively new products, these are planters made from natural materials like corn husks, rice hulls, and bamboo pulp. They can look like plastic or ceramic and will last for a few years before decomposing. Nurseries are starting to carry wider selections, and many more color and size options can be found online.

Hunting for makeshift planters can be a really fun way to spend a weekend afternoon when you have the time. Thrift stores, garage sales, and estate sales are all prime hunting grounds. Just make sure that whatever treasures you find will accommodate a hole being drilled in the bottom for drainage. Here are some ideas for everyday items that can be transformed into curious containers: metal pail, plastic bucket, wooden fruit crate, whiskey or wine barrel, wicker basket, retro food tin, rubber storage bin, old trash can, hollow TV set, ice chest, bathtub.

Wooden containers are also fairly simple to construct if you have a hammer, nails, and a handsaw. Don't be afraid to ask your friends and neighbors if you don't own the right tools. When building your own planter, be sure to use rot-resistant wood. Home improvement stores sell treated lumber, but avoid this chemically treated wood. We don't want to gamble with those chemicals leaching into plants we plan to eat later.

Redwood and cedar are naturally rot-resistant wood choices and work well for planters. Often they are used for fence construction, so leftover fencing can be a great score if it was left unpainted or unstained. More and more cities have salvage building centers too, selling leftover or recycled materials at a low cost. Check with your local lumber yard to see if they have a discard pile where they leave the end cuttings from sold lumber pieces.

Raised Beds

Building raised beds is a more permanent option for growing vegetables, and often a popular one. A low raised bed acts as a designated space for gardening. It lends an organized structure to the garden area that looks tidy and well kept.

A higher raised bed is a great solution if you have compacted or poor soil. The extra space will allow root vegetables like carrots to dig deeper into the bed's fluffy soil. Bringing in good-quality soil to fill raised beds can be a cost savings compared to amending your whole yard. Dog owners favor higher raised beds to prevent their furry friends from marking prized tomatoes.

The height of a raised bed can vary, starting from just a few inches off the ground. Two feet is a very comfortable height that allows plant roots enough depth to dive in, and misses the lifted leg of Howard, our pet greyhound. This is also a fairly comfortable height to kneel down next to or sit along the edge of as you work in the bed.

A raised bed cheaply made with cinder blocks.

Your raised vegetable bed should be no wider than four feet. It gets difficult to reach the middle of the bed for weeding and planting when it gets wider than this. The length can fluctuate to meet your needs, but it is helpful to keep it less than eight feet. Anything longer makes moving a wheelbarrow around cumbersome, and you may begin to feel restricted trying to move between beds for maintenance.

Raised beds can be made from a number of materials: wood (redwood and cedar in particular for their natural rot-resistance), cinder blocks, bricks, bales of straw, flat stones (for stacking), and more.

Instant Garden Patch

Tilling under an area of compacted or weedy soil can create an instant garden patch. The tilling process churns the layers of soil together like a big mixer, creating air pockets that store oxygen and water. You need to pay careful attention to weed and grass seeds that try to sprout from beneath the tilled soil. But with a watchful eye, tilling can work well to loosen the soil up for planting.

As an alternative to tilling a garden patch, you can remove just the layer of lawn and leave the topsoil relatively undisturbed. I have dug out lawn, or sod, by simply using a shovel; it is backbreaking work and the kind of thing you only need to experience once in your life. If you plan on removing a significant amount of lawn, spring for renting a small sod cutter. Like a tiller, this is a big piece of equipment. Garden patches where sod once lived will also require ongoing maintenance to pull weeds and grasses trying to take root once again.

Small tillers and sod cutters can be rented from most home improvement stores for a few hours or a full weekend. Call around in advance to scout the best deal, and make sure you have a large trunk or truck big enough to haul the equipment around. They are going to be very heavy to lift, so bring a friend along for the ride.

Annual tilling is not a very sustainable method, so just till once to break up the initial space. A heavy sod cutter may compress the soil a bit; turning it by hand using a shovel can loosen the ground for planting. Constant disruption of the soil structure will break apart the life and fertility of soil over time. Hand turn in compost with a shovel annually to continually build good soil instead of tilling each year.

A word of caution: start small. Keep dreaming big, but till under or remove sod from only a small area at a time. Next year, if things go well, expand the patch by tilling under more grass. Just be careful to not bite off more than you can chew. Give yourself the best chance of success by picking a reasonable starting size. If you are still fighting the urge to till everything under, combine a partly tilled area with a small container garden. You can still push the limits of your gardening aspirations without making drastically permanent changes.

Community Gardens

If you have more gardening ambition than you simply have space for, a community garden plot could be the answer to your greenest dreams. They are as diverse and eclectic as the people who dig there, and can be found in urban, suburban, and even rural areas. Various organizations such as local neighborhood groups, churches, schools, or public agencies like the city parks department manage the gardens. Typically the plots are used for food production, although a neighborhood may have one just for flowers. Often the groups charge a nominal annual fee for a plot of land, providing tools and a water source for those who garden there.

Originally, most community gardens were created as a way to connect poorer communities to a source of affordable, healthy foods. The gardens tend to grow in numbers during times of economic distress—the Great Depression, World War II, etc.— and shrink a bit as people recover. Currently, community gardens are rising in popularity for a more complex set of reasons. The sustainable-living movement, economic recession, and questions about the industrialized food system have increased consumer demand for organic and locally sourced food products. Fewer people have access to an in-ground gardening space as our cities become more efficient, yet denser.

It is not uncommon to encounter a community gardener who also has a home garden. They may be utilizing a community garden because they have a heavy reliance on homegrown food and need a larger gardening space. Perhaps they have formed a social community at the garden and enjoy being in an engaging atmosphere surrounded by like-minded people.

These diverse gardens also act as much-needed green spaces. They break up the concrete jungles and invite people

to linger a little longer in a calming, refreshing space. They have been found to reduce crime rates in their area, and they offer the opportunity to make communities stronger. People of different generations and ethnic backgrounds can cross divides to share knowledge and resources with each other. They can exchange produce, as well as tips on pest control.

Ethnically diverse neighborhoods often have many different types of vegetables and growing methods all in one place. For example, Asian immigrants might construct a trellis over their plot to grow squash, shading Asian greens growing underneath. Native Americans use a gardening layout called the Three Sisters. Mounded soil is planted with corn, squash, and beans. The corn acts as a trellis for the beans while the squash shades the soil underneath, protecting it from evaporation and helping with water retention. Traditional African gardens are not laid out in a grid, but rather plants are grouped together to maximize the growing space.

You can pick up some very interesting tips on how to maximize your plot's production by tuning into these different practices and talking with your plot neighbors. Exchange recipes and seeds, and start bridging the divide that can often exist in diverse communities.

Depending on the community garden, there is often a waiting list for a plot. Be patient and focus on container gardening at home while you wait for your number to be called. Often community gardens offer annual seed swaps and work parties. There are usually community garden

meetings and periodic work parties to keep the grounds up. See if you can get involved early to start learning the ropes before you actually get your own space.

The use of pesticides is generally discouraged in community gardens, so most will be organic spaces. There will almost always be a compost system onsite where gardeners can dispose of plant waste. Gardeners are expected to use their share of the finished compost and leave enough for everyone else. Tools and water should be provided, and the gardens are often fenced in for security.

Because community gardens can be managed by such a wide range of organizations, your best bet for finding the closest plot can be through your local garden store or the American Community Garden Association (ACGA). The ACGA also has a wonderful Listserv you can join to get advice or feedback on gardening issues.

Plot sizes vary depending on the community garden. You can always invite a friend to share your plot if you are not using the whole space. Alternatively, if your space is too small, see if you can work out a trade agreement with neighbor gardeners. Maybe you don't have room for a zucchini plant, but you can trade another gardener some beans in exchange for a zucchini from their plant.

Companion planting lettuce with onions lets you grow more with less space.

ALL ABOUT SOIL

All great gardens begin with great soil. Period. Unfortunately, not all of us are lucky enough to have great soil when we decide to begin a garden. In fact, most of us, it seems, get stuck with heavy clay or nutrient-sapped, dried-out dirt. While you wait for your compost bin to get going, you may want to consider shelling out some clams for a load of nice soil to be mixed in with your current soil (or if you're going the container route, buy enough bags to get your pots filled, utilizing the compost pile later). As a poor beginning gardener with heavy clay soil, I opted to buy one bag of quality compost, which made all the difference for my vegetables to thrive.

The soil in our gardens is home to important microscopic life-forms called microorganisms. These little bacteria and fungi have an important, mutually beneficial relationship with plants. If you want strong, healthy plants you need to have a strong, healthy community of microorganisms in your soil. Let's take a quick peek into this complicated and invisible world to better understand what our plants want.

Plants need nutrients from the soil that they cannot gather themselves. Therefore, these little microorganisms work through the soil, gathering important plant nutrients. Meanwhile, the plants are working on photosynthesis—absorbing sunlight and transforming it into sugar.

The microorganisms make their way to the plants' roots for the exchange. They give the plants valuable nutrients, and the plants give them food in the way of excess sugar. Both parties get something they need to survive and thrive.

A balanced soil is one that makes a really cozy home for both plants and microorganisms. Typically this begins with the following ratios: 25 percent air, 25 percent water, 45 percent soil, and 5 percent organic matter.

The air in soil keeps the consistency light and fluffy. Plant roots can dig deep for stability and access to water. Air space also provides room for microorganisms to live and holds the oxygen they need to survive. Having air in your soil also makes little pockets to store water until needed.

Just as you do not want your soil to be too dry, you do not want your soil to be too wet—plants can drown in too much water. The appropriate amount of water ensures your plants can drink when they are thirsty. Those little microorganisms will also need a drink now and then to survive.

Balanced soil has good tilth, which means it has a rich brown color, feels light and fluffy, and has a nice spongelike quality. Another term for this spongy, good soil is garden loam. You should be able to squeeze the soil tightly and have it stay clumped together when you open your hand. Good soil structure is composed of 40 percent sand, 40 percent silt, and 20 percent clay. If the soil does not stay together, it may be too sandy. If you can roll the soil into a long worm shape, you may have too much clay.

Organic material is what feeds all those microorganisms. The more food they have, the more they multiply and have enough energy to run around collecting nutrients to trade with your plants. Organic material comes in the way of compost, which is made from manure, food scraps, leaves, straw, and other natural materials. Basically, anything that came from the earth that will break down and decompose over time can be considered organic material.

Aim for a minimum of 5 percent organic material, but you can go as high as 8 percent for vegetable gardening. Vegetable plants typically need more nutrients to produce food than ornamental plants, meaning they need more microorganisms working underground to help them thrive. It is possible to have too much of a good thing, though. Going overboard with organic material can result in a nutrient overload, which would actually harm your plants.

Buying Soil

You can run out and buy good garden soil if your garden is soil challenged and your budget allows. Start small with a container garden, go a little bigger with raised beds, or decide to blanket the whole garden patch with a thick layer of fluffy over-the-counter garden loam. Think about buying only enough soil for the area you are planting this season. Maybe next summer your whole garden plot will be filled, but if you are only starting out with a few tomatoes, get enough soil for just those guys.

You can buy garden soil from your local plant shop, nursery, home improvement center, and large-scale local soil suppliers.

The local garden shop will often have the most knowledgeable staff who can help you find the perfect soil mix for your needs, offering various-sized bags of different soil mixes. A home improvement center can be a slightly cheaper option that also sells small quantities, but they often will not have as wide a selection or as knowledgeable a staff. Soil suppliers are the cheapest option because you typically

Good soil has a spongelike consistency when squeezed.

buy in large quantities. Start talking to your friends and neighbors who are also interested in gardening. If you can all go in together, perhaps you can get a better

Collect fall leaves to use as browns in your compost all year.

soil mix for growing vegetables so she can steer you toward mixes with lots of compost. Often places sell an organic garden loam that is the perfect consistency for growing vegetables.

Soil for use in a container garden is a little different from that used for raised-bed or in-ground gardening. Container, or potting, soil will actually be called a soilless mix. It is lightweight, making the containers easier to move around. It is also highly absorbent to keep water in the pots for as long as possible. Choose a soil type that specifically notes that it is appropriate for containers. As the plants use the nutrients in the soilless mix, you may need to add a little more of the mix annually.

Making Your Own Soil

It is possible to get good soil over time without dropping tons of cash. If your soil balance is off, whether it is too grainy or has too much clay, adding organic material will help it balance out over time. We can't all afford truckloads of perfect soil, so look for free sources of organic materials to make your own.

Plants extract nutrients from the soil each season, so vegetable gardens need help replenishing these stores of nutrients. A little planning now will help you stay on top of your plants' soil needs every year. Some easy, low-cost methods of restoring soil quality are lasagna layering, planting cover crops, adding organic fertilizers, and creating your own compost system.

Pick a method or two that work for you—but don't feel like you need to do everything under the sun to build your

deal. The truck will probably only dump at one location, then everyone can come over and fill up their buckets or vehicles to bring home their share. Alternatively, you can fill up your car if you don't have a large enough order for a delivery. It will save you the cost of delivery, which is not always cost effective for small quantities.

Garden soil mixes usually include a balanced soil mix (sand, silt, and clay) and a nice dose of organic material, or compost. If you know your soil is currently too sandy or too heavy with clay, mention that to the salesperson so she can help balance it. Tell her you need a soil. For example, when I start a new garden, often I am working with pretty poor soil. I use a combination of lasagna layers and adding in a mix of organic fertilizers to get the soil back on the path to recovery. For an established garden, I use cover crops and turn in homemade compost once a year to replenish what my vegetables have taken out of the soil. George Washington, an avid farmer, used a combination of cover crops and livestock manure added a couple times a year. Experiment to find out what works best on your homestead.

Lasagna Layers

Also called sheet mulching, lasagna layers are thick layers of different organic materials piled on top of one another in the garden and allowed to decompose in place. This is a great option if you have really poor soil or want to create an instant garden patch without digging up sod.

It's easy to find free or cheap sources of organic materials, and you will end up with fluffy, nutrient-rich soil after a few short months. Fall is a great time to make the layers, so they can break down over the winter. You can plant directly into the area in the spring, without any tilling needed.

If you are layering over sod, begin by placing large sheets of cardboard over your future garden area. It looks weird, but it will kill the grass and weeds by blocking them from sunlight. The cardboard will be hidden by the lasagna layers piled on top and will eventually decompose completely. After getting the cardboard into place, get it very wet with a hose. This

softens it up a bit and invites the worms to come up and start munching. If you are layering over poor soil instead of grass, skip the cardboard altogether and begin making your layers.

Layers of different organic material should be thickly applied, with the whole lasagna being about two feet in thickness. Let the layers sit for a few months as the worms and microorganisms do their work to decompose everything.

Here is a short list of some ingredients you can use for your layers:

- Talk to ranchers at your local farmers' market about picking up a free carload of cow manure from their farms.
- Ask your coffee shop if you can collect their used coffee grounds once a week. Coffee grounds used alone in large quantities could raise your soil's acidity levels, but when mixed with food scraps they can make some great compost.
- Most cities have a leaf collection service in the fall and will dump a load for free. Inquire with the city or ask neighbors to give you their bagged leaves. Often they need to pay to get rid of them.
- Local arborists send pruned branches and cut trees through a wood chipper, then pay to dump the wood load somewhere. Call around and see if an arborist would be interested in dumping a load of wood chips for free at your place. Be sure to request they do not dump chips from diseased trees.

Using a combination of ingredients will create a richer soil after they have broken down. For example, start with a layer of coffee grounds and add manure from a local rancher for the next layer. Then spread a thick layer of dried leaves over the manure layer. In areas with a lot of foot traffic, like where my fruit trees and berry bushes are planted, I finished my lasagna layers off with wood chips from the local arborist. They take several years to break down and give the yard a clean, tidy appearance.

While you are inside during the winter months poring over seed catalogs, your garden is busily working away. In a few months, the lasagna garden layers will sink down significantly, to about 25 percent of their original size. You will be giving microorganisms plenty to chew on, space in the soil to thrive, and all those layers of mulch will hold in water during dry spells.

Cover Crops

Certain plants are considered to be green manure, which means you plant them for the nutrients they add into the soil rather than planting them to eat. When the soil needs a break from growing vegetables, you plant cover crops to restore the nutrients. Some types of cover crops can be grown at any time of the year, while others should be planted only in certain seasons.

I like using cover crops in the fall, when I am ready for a gardening break. I plant the cover crop seeds into the garden beds right after I have pulled out the last of my vegetables. They grow on their own through the winter, and I turn them into the soil in the spring before they begin to flower.

You can choose from legume or grain cover crops. After turning in the legume cover crops before they flower, the plant leaves and stems break down and add nitrogen back into the soil. Grain cover crops do not add nitrogen, but they still add organic matter to the soil to keep things fluffy and help with water retention.

Here is a short list of some popular legume cover crops:

Crimson clover
Fava beans
Austrian field peas
Hairy vetch

Here is a short list of some popular grain cover crops:

Buckwheat
Barley
Oats
Rye

Your local garden store or extension services office can recommend an even longer list of cover crops. The seeds are cheap and the effort is minimal, since you can just plant and walk away from them. The little extra effort in the fall always pays off for my garden in the spring.

Fertilizer

To quickly add nutrients back into your garden soil, consider an application of organic fertilizer. You can mix up your own blend as you learn about the individual needs of your garden plot. Here is a balanced recipe to get you started:

Organic fertilizer ingredients (clockwise from top): alfalfa meal, lime, rock phosphate, kelp.

4 parts lime
4 parts alfalfa meal (N)
3 parts rock phosphate (P)
2 parts kelp or greensand (K)

Lime is a naturally occurring element that works toward balancing your soil's pH level. It should be added to acidic soils to bring the levels down to a happy medium for vegetable growing.

Alfalfa meal is an organic source of nitrogen, which your plants need to grow thick leaves and foliage. It encourages photosynthesis capabilities that in turn boost the microorganism content in the soil. Consider adding an extra dose for vegetables whose leaves you eat, like collards, kale, chard, and lettuce.

Phosphate benefits plant root development and increases the amount plants flower. More flowers mean more fruit! This can be especially helpful for root vegetables like carrots and parsnips. Rock phosphate is collected from phosphoric rock deposits in areas like Florida.

Greensand washes up on the shorelines and is the remnant of ancient kelp beds. Kelp is very high in potassium, which benefits all-around plant health and development.

The mixture does not need to be precise. I mix mine in a large bucket and sprinkle it onto the garden beds right before planting, then turn in with a spade. Too much fertilizer might shock your plants, so take it easy and just lightly dust the planting areas. I use a one-quart canning jar of fertilizer for roughly a twenty-square-foot area—a little goes a long way! Store the unused fertilizer mix in a covered container in a cool, dry place. Give it a mix each time you use it to ensure heavier particles are not buried in the bottom of the bucket.

COMPOSTING

As organic material decomposes over time, what is left behind is known as compost. The end product of compost is called humus, a loamy soil material that smells like rich earth and is very dark, almost black, in color.

Humus is packed full of millions of microorganisms that have been busily breaking down the organic material. It is also packed full of rich nutrients that your plants crave. Because of all these fabulous attributes, you should get a composting system going as soon as you decide to start a garden, to build up the soil into good tilth.

Creating your own compost system has so many benefits:

- Reducing what goes into landfills
- Minimizing your carbon footprint by composting on site rather than having a fuel-powered truck haul it away
- Creating a continuous source of highly valuable organic material
- Saving money by reducing your need to buy commercial compost and organic fertilizers

There are tons of different methods for composting, so surely one will fit your needs and space requirements. It can be as complex as a three-bin outdoor system where you produce wheelbarrows of compost every couple months, or as simple as a plastic bin under your kitchen sink that houses worms that eat your garbage. Whatever system you choose, get your compost on!

Compost: The Goods

There is a lot of talk about compost in the gardening world, and here is an example of why it's so important. I built raised beds at our first house and sprang for a large load of garden soil to fill them. The first year in that garden was great, with a good second year, but a mediocre third season. I realized the soil had become really sandy and compacted by that point. The vegetables were using up all the nutrients, and I needed to be adding in more compost each season to replenish the food supply.

The moral of this story is that even if you buy great soil today, over the years you need to keep developing it with new sources of organic matter. The microorganisms need fresh food sources, and the nutrients need replenishing as they are consumed by your plants. Building good soil may be free, but it takes time to break down compost to feed your plants. Even before you build the garden beds, you may want to make sure you have started a compost pile to feed your plants in a few months.

All organic matter contains some mixture of carbon and nitrogen, which decomposes over time. How quickly it will decompose depends on the ratio of carbon to nitrogen. The decomposers, whose job it is to feed on organic waste, prefer an overall ratio of thirty parts carbon to one part nitrogen, or a 30/1 ratio.

Food waste typically contains a high level of nitrogen. In the compost world,

Turn your compost pile to energize microorganisms with fresh oxygen.

we call this stuff greens. There is carbon in there as well, but at lower levels. Greens are packed full of valuable nutrients, but a compost pile that consists of just greens would take forever to break down because it doesn't achieve this 30/1 ratio. It also ends up as a big stinky mess.

This is why it is important to mix in lots of browns, which are organic matter that has a higher carbon level. Browns come in the form of dried leaves, straw, wood chips, shredded newspaper, and other materials. When we mix the high-carbon browns together with the high-nitrogen greens, they create a carbon/nitrogen–balanced compost pile that will break down faster with no foul odors.

Livestock manure from cows, horses, goats, and poultry has valuable nutrients and is considered to be a green compost ingredient due to its high nitrogen level. Soiled poultry bedding can be a great and continual source of browns that have a nice dash of greens already mixed in. Dog and cat manure should not be added to the compost pile because it can carry harmful pathogens that are difficult to kill off.

The microbes eating this organic waste are tiny creatures and therefore need to eat things in tiny pieces. If you throw a whole zucchini into your compost pile, it will eventually break down. But chopping it into smaller pieces will help it break down faster.

As discussed earlier, microorganisms need both oxygen and water to survive. A lack of oxygen means the microbes will work slower and the compost will start

getting pungent due to anaerobic conditions. Turning the compost pile throws fresh oxygen back into the pile, allowing air circulation and reenergizing those microbes.

Wood chips can be used as browns for compost, but they decompose slowly.

One way to check whether your compost heap is breaking down quickly is to check its temperature. Use a long thermometer found at hardware and feed stores to read down into the center of the pile. An ideal pile will reach a temperature range of 130 to 150 degrees Fahrenheit. This tells you that energy is being created from the microorganisms breaking down the waste. If the temperature is lower than 130 degrees, give the pile a turn and check that you have a good carbon/nitrogen balance. The compost will be finished breaking down when the pile has cooled and a humus texture has developed. Finished compost can be turned into your garden soil when needed.

This compost pile is actively breaking down at 135 degrees Fahrenheit.

I typically throw things onto my compost pile in layers, keeping each layer no thicker than about six inches. Thicker layers cause the microbes to work really hard to move between materials. I empty my kitchen scraps once a week, around the time I plan to clean my chicken coop or rake up some leaves. The food waste gets thrown on the pile, and I immediately top it off with a thick layer of used chicken bedding in the form of straw or dried leaves I collected in the fall. Once a month I turn the pile, giving the microbes a nice breath of fresh air.

I am not super anal about the carbon-nitrogen levels. With experience, you will begin to learn when you have added too much carbon or too much nitrogen. A good rule of thumb for beginners is to add one part greens to two parts browns. Always top the pile off with browns to keep unwanted critters from being attracted to the food. The pile needs to have some moisture for the microbes to keep working, so you may need to sprinkle it with water in the heat of summer if it dries out. Cover the pile with a tarp to keep it from getting too wet in rainy weather.

Single-Bin System

Retailers sell a variety of commercially made composting bins, so you have some decisions to make—another fun reason to sift through garden catalogs and visit the plant store! I recommend avoiding compost bins you need to turn with a hand crank, because they can get very difficult to maneuver when full. I have had good results with black-plastic domed compost bins, which absorb heat and keep the temperatures inside toasty.

Currently I have a homemade compost bin that has been working very well, and was acquired at my favorite price—free. I rounded up four wooden pallets from a nearby department store. I assembled them into a four-sided bin with one side acting as a door. I hinged the door rustically to one side with rope so I can move it open and closed when needed. The pallet sides allow air to circulate evenly around the pile, and I give things a good stir periodically. It's not fancy, but it's a good example of how almost anything can be used to make a simple bin.

Multi-Bin System

The composting method that gives you the largest supply of rich humus is something commonly referred to as a three-bin system, although the concept can be applied to any number of compost bins, depending on your needs. If three bins are too much for your needs, consider a smaller, two-bin system. The urban farm I volunteer with has a never-ending supply of dried leaves, used straw, food scraps from local restaurants, and plant waste from the vegetable beds. In this case, we use a ten-bin system to generate lots of compost continually.

Regardless of the final number of bins you use, each bin typically has four sides and they sit next to each other. The first bin gets filled with fresh organic material until it is full. After it has been sitting for a few weeks, the contents of that bin then need to be tossed with a pitchfork into the empty middle bin next to it. This aerates the compost heap and jump-starts a second round of decomposition.

Begin to fill the newly emptied first bin again with new compost materials. Meanwhile, the original pile sits in the middle bin, continuing to break down. As the first bin fills up a second time, the piles get moved again. If you are using a three-bin system, the mostly broken down humus in the middle bin gets moved to the third bin. The full first bin gets tossed into the newly emptied middle bin. The first bin is now empty again and ready to be filled with fresh compost materials.

By the time that first bin gets filled again, the original compost pile in the third bin should be fully broken down into

Three-bin system with fresh compost material (right), partially decomposed material (middle), and finished compost ready for the garden (left).

humus. It's time to spread this good compost into the garden beds, freeing up the third bin. With this system, you always have a bin to add new compost materials to, one that is partially broken down, and one that holds finished compost.

Compost bins can be made of a huge range of materials. Wood works nicely for these larger, multi-bin systems. I have seen some really fancy bins that were constructed with cedar and have doors that swing open, allowing you to get in there with your pitchfork to toss things around. Whatever your material choice, plan for good air circulation and make it easy to access.

As mentioned earlier, I prefer a very rustic, and fabulously free, version using wood pallets. They are assembled on their sides to create three side-by-side bins with rope holding the front pallet in place so they can be moved opened and closed when needed. Keeping the front pallet door roped in place allows me to pile the compost heap right up to the top of the bin. I throw a tarp on the top of each pile, with a heavy rock to keep it in place, which prevents rain from making the compost pile too wet.

Wood pallets can be found all over town if you keep your eyes peeled. I have gathered most of mine from department stores—in the back, where the deliveries are made. There are always plenty to be found at home improvement and large feed stores as well. If a store owner wants you to buy the pallets, say thanks but no thanks and keep looking.

Vermicomposting

Composting with worms is the perfect answer for apartment dwellers who want to create their own compost or simply want to reduce their waste. You will be shocked how little garbage goes to a landfill each week once you get into the habit of redirecting your food waste. Amazingly, something that you once saw as worthless—food scraps—becomes another coin in the compost piggy bank. In a couple months, you'll be cashing in.

Worms chew food scraps and turn them into rich compost.

Using a worm bin allows composting worms to eat waste and leave worm castings (i.e., worm manure) behind. It also invites in aerobic, or oxygen-producing, microorganisms of all microscopic shapes and sizes to work on breaking those particles down into humus. A good worm-bin system allows the good guys to do the work and keeps the bad guys at bay.

Who are the bad guys? Anaerobic microorganisms, which stink—literally. They are the ones that live in your garbage bag and make it gag-inducing. They are still breaking down that material into valuable nutrients, but they smell awful, making aerobic guys more attractive to composters.

Here is what you need to create and maintain your worm operation: a bin, bedding, food waste, and composting worms. Let's break down what that all means.

First, the Bin

Typically your choice for the container is between wood and plastic. Metal can potentially rust, although if you keep a close watch to ensure there is no standing water and find a way to punch in some good aeration holes, you could experiment with metal. Wood works best for aeration, but it is heavy and requires some serious tools for assemblage—like a power saw to cut the wood. It will last about two to three years before the moisture breaks it down. Avoid pressure-treated wood, which can poison the worms. Plastic is cheap, plentiful, light, and easy to put together with makeshift tools. It does not breathe as well as wood, so make extra aeration holes and monitor any standing water issues.

Worms breathe through their skin, which needs to be moist in order for them to capture the air they need and secrete waste. Too much water, though, in the way of standing water, will drown the poor guys. Good aeration will make sure the worms don't drown. It also prevents the bin from overheating as the worms work the materials inside. The most

Drill extra aeration holes in plastic worm bins.

noticeable problem with a lack of aeration is an unpleasant garbage smell. Without proper oxygen reaching your food waste, anaerobic microorganisms take over, and we all know we don't want those.

Punch or drill holes into your container along the top or the sides to keep air moving through. Make the holes about one inch in diameter and put some wire mesh over them. Worms like to stay in dark, warm places so they are not likely to leave the box, but you want to keep unwanted critters like flies from getting in the bin.

Shredded newspaper makes excellent worm bedding.

If you are a single person or a couple, a bin roughly three to four square feet in size should be ample. A family of four is well suited to a bin roughly six square feet in size. A bin with a one-foot depth and lots of surface area is best, as opposed to a deeper, narrower bin. A shallow box will allow worms to eat more food and will allow more oxygen to reach the contents.

Consider a bin that is 2 x 2 feet and 1 foot in depth or 3 x 2 feet and 1 foot in depth.

Be resourceful, as always, when acquiring your bin. Dumpster dive for old plastic containers or gather wood scraps big enough for each side of your bin. Things like dresser drawers and old toy chests can be refashioned into excellent worm digs.

Next, Make the Bed

The worm bin needs bedding in addition to food scraps so the worms have a nice place to call home. The bedding creates pockets for oxygen, holds in heat, and absorbs smells by counterbalancing the nitrogen-heavy food scraps. Bedding can come from a variety of materials: dried leaves, livestock manure, straw, coconut fiber, wood chips, and shredded newspaper.

You don't have to choose just one. Manure on its own can be pretty smelly. Coconut fiber can be expensive to buy from the garden center on a regular basis. Dried leaves are only plentiful at one time of the year. Think about adding these seasonal or pricey options to other readily available ones, like shredded newspaper.

Wood chips last a long time and provide large air pockets for oxygen. It can be easy to separate the chips from the fine black humus when you want to use the composted good stuff. Straw mixed with some chicken manure is a constantly producing bedding source if you have backyard chickens.

For the modern homesteader, shredded newspaper is the most commonly used bedding material. It is free, plentiful, and a way to reuse something that would otherwise get recycled. Shredded newspaper works great with other materials or just on its own. The inks are nontoxic and safe for composting because they are now all vegetable based. For homesteaders in apartments or with small plots, newspaper may be the easiest and cheapest route.

Whatever bedding you decide on, add a handful of plain-Jane soil when you add in large quantities of new bedding. This gives the worms grit material, which they will hold in their little worm gizzards to mash their food up. Worms don't have teeth, so these rough particles in the gizzard break things apart so they can digest them.

Set the Table

Tons of organic material can be used for worm food. The short list of things to avoid includes bones and meat, which can attract yucky critters like mice and rats. Pet feces are also not allowed, as they can carry unwanted pathogens. Nonorganic waste, like rubber bands and plastic, and bioplastics, like biodegradable forks, will never break down and should not be added. Everything else is fair game.

Common food waste for compost are vegetable and fruit scraps, moldy bread, smashed eggshells (so they break down easier), coffee grounds, yogurt, spent cheese, and on and on. You can also throw in other nonfood items that are made from organic materials, like tea bags, cheesecloth, coffee filters, tissues, and paper napkins.

You do not need to feed your worms every day, although you could if that is

Feed composting worms a wide array of food scraps.

easier for you. If you have one of those small countertop compost containers, you can empty it once a week, every couple days, or whenever it just happens to fill up. It really depends on your preference, the convenience of the location of the bin, and how quickly you accumulate food scraps.

My worm bin is outside, attached to my bantam chicken coop. It's a longer walk to the bin, so I keep a tight-fitting compost bucket under my sink next to the trash can and recycling bin. The lid keeps the anaerobic smells contained while the bin is full in the house. I empty the compostable materials into the worm bin once a week, when I routinely take out the garbage and recycling. I clean my bantam chicken coop once a week as well, so I just add in the used bedding when I dump the kitchen scraps.

Enter Worms

The worm bin has been constructed, the bedding accumulated, and food scraps are ready for feeding. It's now time to bring home some good composting worms.

Worms are not all created equal when it comes to eating garbage. Some worms are excellent for working their way through the earth, and others excel at eating waste and converting it into compost. To complicate things further, different types of worms can reproduce faster than others. You want your worm population to be as abundant as the food scraps you feed it so things break down quickly. And finally, some worms will hate you lifting the lid and messing up their homes while others are laid back about the whole deal. You want the laid-back variety that work away, don't mind occasional disturbances, and reproduce quickly.

To save you some researching, I advise you get your composting hands on some red wigglers. These little guys have variations on their common name, but the actual species is *Eisenia fetida*. Yes, worms, like plants and other living things, have crazy Latin names. Redworms, red wigglers, and red hybrids are all common names for these worms.

With the increasing popularity of worm composting, red wigglers are becoming easier and easier to acquire. Plant shops, nurseries, and bait shops often have them

Red wigglers move into their new home.

in stock. You can find them through online sources (try http://vermicomposters.com). Or maybe you already have a buddy who composts with worms and would love to trade a bag o' worms for a six-pack of something cool and tasty.

Wherever you get your red wigglers, try to start with no less than one pound of worms, which should be around 1,000 worms. Some places may sell bedrun worms, which means they are mixed ages. Others may specifically sell young breeders, which are smaller and lighter in weight but ready to reproduce like crazy. In either case, give it a little time and they will multiply. Eventually they self-manage their population, reproducing only enough worms to have a 2:1 ratio of worms to food. That means one pound of worms will eat a half pound of food scraps per day.

Moving Day

You have your bin, bedding, food scraps, and worms. Now it's time to put it all together and move the worms into their new home.

In a separate container, mix the bedding with a couple handfuls of soil. Now add in three parts water weight to one part bedding weight. That means for every one pound of bedding, mix in three pounds of water. If that is too complicated and you don't own a scale, just mix in enough water so the bedding is damp but not soggy—it's just right when you can squeeze a drop or two of water from the bedding. If you are using a plastic bin, use a little less water, as plastic inhibits evaporation.

Place the bedding evenly in the worm bin, reserving a bit to use at the end for topping things off. Spread the worms evenly over the bedding and give them a few minutes to dig down. Next, add food scraps and bury them into the bedding. Use the reserved bedding to cover the scraps. Put the cover into place and let the worms do their work.

Worm Bin Maintenance

As you feed your worms, bury food waste into one spot at a time. Rotate to a new spot when you deposit the next batch of food waste. When you can no longer dig down into the bedding enough to bury food waste, or when most of the contents of the bin are black castings, it's time to add more bedding and potentially harvest the vermicompost. This can take anywhere from one to three months, depending on how much kitchen waste you feed the worms and how big the bin is.

To harvest your compost, push everything over to one side of the bin. Add new bedding to the open area and bury some food waste there. Give the worms a couple days, and they will make their way over to the new food deposit. You can then remove the compost from the bin and use it in the garden to build your soil quality. You will lose a few worms when you harvest, but the remaining ones will multiply quickly.

If the bedding gets too flattened, fluff it up to break up the compaction and keep air continually circulating. Keeping a garden fork next to the bin makes it easier to fluff the bedding when needed.

PLANNING THE GARDEN

One of the first steps in deciding what to grow is taking a good look at what you currently eat. Think about what you buy from the grocery store or farmers' market on a regular basis and what you enjoy eating at home. Pore over seed catalogs for new varieties of your favorite fruits and vegetables, like purple carrots or white watermelons. You want to grow things you are already used to eating and branch out from there with a few new vegetables to try.

My husband and I eat salad almost every night with dinner, so we have a mixture of mesclun greens growing pretty much year-round. I balance out my low iron levels by planting and eating lots of kale and spinach for an energy boost. One prolific zucchini plant is enough to keep any baker busy all summer making moist brownies, breakfast breads, and cookies. Planting things you already enjoy means you get the most from your gardening efforts and little goes to waste.

Planning the coming season's crops is a gardener's favorite winter pastime, entertaining us on chilly afternoons. But no matter what time of year you begin, there is usually something just around the corner you can plant. Make a little list of the things you want to plant, prep the soil, and sip some tea as you wait for planting time.

Perennial versus Annual

Some plants come back every year and some you need to plant again each year. The ones that never go away are called perennials. These are things like berry bushes, fruit trees, artichoke plants, and asparagus. Most vegetables, though, are considered annuals, meaning you need to plant them from seed or transplant them from starts every year.

The good news about annuals is that at the end of the season many will produce seeds that you can then collect and replant the next year (provided they aren't terminator-style seeds, which are worthless after one growing season—do your research!). You will become better at seed-saving as you get more experienced.

Harvesting basil for a quick pesto dinner.

Sick of zucchini? Try a summer squash like a yellow crookneck heirloom.

Easy to Difficult Plants

Plants that are considered easy are often ones that can handle slight drought and are considered to be light feeders, meaning they do not consume a high level of nutrients from the soil. Easy vegetables are not overly sensitive to slight temperature changes. They can be direct-sown into the ground rather than grown from seed and transplanted, and they often ripen quickly. Vegetables like snap peas, snow peas, zucchini, lettuce, arugula, and radishes are great choices for the beginner gardener.

Moderate vegetables require slightly more care than these übereasy vegetables. Carrots, broccoli, beets, and bush and pole beans need a slightly closer eye on them. Broccoli, for example, often attracts aphids, which are a problem pest. Carrots need to be sown neatly and thinned carefully as they mature. They say the best fertilizer is the gardener's shadow, so work a daily garden stroll into your routine to spot pests and take care of maintenance issues early on.

Higher-maintenance vegetables are the divas of the vegetable garden. They require well-fertilized soils and regular, deep watering. They are particular about temperature and can be prone to more pests and diseases. They are not impossible to grow by any means, but they do need more attention. In return they are tasty performers that will steal the garden show. (Sorry, beets!) These divas are plants like tomatoes, peppers, eggplants, and sweet corn.

Climate substantially affects your ability to grow plants successfully. Areas with

It saves cash to avoid buying new seed packets every year. Often, when you buy a packet of lettuce seeds, for example, it includes upward of 200 little seeds. Most likely you will not use a full packet in one season anyway, and the rest can be stored until next year.

Consider planting a mix of perennials and annuals in your garden. The annuals are your summer workhorses that load you up with produce, whereas the perennials are safety plants you can count on every year for a harvest once established. And don't be discouraged if you are working with containers only. Many berry bushes happily live in containers, as do several fruit trees such as lemons and figs. I've even seen columnar apple cultivars fit for containers; they grow only a few feet in height on a central branch that produces lots of fruit.

Plant	Easy	Medium	Difficult
Artichoke		x	
Arugula	x		
Asian greens		x	
Asparagus			x
Basil		x	
Beans, bush		x	
Beans, pole		x	
Beets		x	
Broccoli		x	
Brussels sprouts			x
Cabbage			x
Carrots		x	
Celery	x		
Chard		x	
Cilantro		x	
Collard greens	x		
Corn			x
Cucumber	x		
Eggplant			x
Garlic	x		
Kale	x		
Kohlrabi		x	
Leeks		x	
Lettuce	x		
Melons		x	
Onions, bulbs	x		
Onions, green	x		
Parsley		x	
Parsnips		x	
Peas, snap	x		
Peas, snow	x		
Peppers			x
Potatoes	x		
Pumpkin	x		
Radish	x		
Shallots	x		
Spinach	x		
Summer squash	x		
Tomatoes			x
Winter squash	x		
Zucchini	x		

Harvesting heirloom tomatoes, the divas of vegetable gardening.

mild summers can make it challenging to grow heat-loving plants like tomatoes and eggplants. Southern regions get way too hot way too quickly, making it difficult to successfully grow cold-weather crops like kale, beets, and lettuces.

Checking your local farmers' market will show you what farmers in your area are able to grow and when. Talking to your local plant shop will also help you decide whether you should attempt different vegetable crops. Many garden shops and local extension service offices offer free vegetable calendars that advise you what to plant and when. Better yet, they often recommend varieties particularly well-suited for your area.

PLANTING PLAN: THE YARDLESS

One of the easiest things to grow in the world, even in the smallest of garden spaces, is a perennial herb garden. Many herbs are considered drought tolerant and will provide you with evergreen foliage and access to fresh culinary flavor year-round. Think of them as hardworking houseplants. The minimum requirement is a windowsill.

Pick some combination of herbs like oregano, chives, rosemary, sage, marjoram, and thyme. Most can thrive in partial to full sun. For a fully shaded windowsill, choose both curly and flat-leafed, or Italian, parsley. Chives, thyme, lemon balm, and mint are also good heavy-shade options. Perhaps mojitos will become the specialty drink at your dinner parties.

Each herb has a few varieties to choose from, especially if you get your plants from a good local nursery. Think about the different colors and textures to find an eye-pleasing combination. Sure, you are planting these to cook with, but take this as an opportunity to up the visual appeal of your garden space. Scout out some variegated thyme varieties that sport green-and-yellow foliage or maybe white stripes on dark green leaves. That would contrast nicely with a dark purple sage. Add lime-green oregano in there to make the whole thing pop.

In the spring, try your hand at planting some annuals in between the perennial plantings. The most common annual herbs are basil, cilantro, and parsley, all of which really jazz up summer dishes.

Continual harvesting ensures that basil doesn't bolt.

Make sure to pick the leaves off these guys often, though. When the temperatures rise, they get the urge to bolt, meaning they will develop flowers and go to seed. Unfortunately, that abruptly ends your harvest, as the leaves become too bitter tasting. Constant picking forces the plants to continue producing leaves instead of flowers. Stagger the planting of these herbs as well to prevent everything from bolting at the same time.

In addition to your herb garden, get your hands on a hanging planter—either purchased from the store or made with

Plant Terminology

As you research which vegetable varieties to grow this year, here are some terms you will see often on seed packets and such:

- **Cold-tolerant:** These plants prefer to grow in cooler temperatures. If you live in a hot climate, this may mean you can grow this vegetable through the winter, but it will not do well in the summer. If you live in a mild climate, you may be able to grow it all year.
- **Heat-loving:** Tomatoes, eggplants, melons, and peppers are examples of heat-loving plants. Their growth will be stunted and your harvest meager if they do not get warm enough. These are great options for those living in southern areas. For the northerners, consider growing these plants in dark containers, allowing the sun to absorb into the soil and heat things up.
- **Quick-ripening:** New varieties are being developed every year that shorten the growing needs of various vegetables. If the growing season is short in your area, think about choosing varieties that have been cultivated over time to develop fruit more quickly.
- **Overwintering:** Vegetables that prefer slightly cooler temperatures, like broccoli and cabbage, have specific varieties that take a longer period to grow and mature. These are ones you would plant in the fall to then enjoy in the early spring. They can tolerate the cold of winter, which improves their flavor, and can still mature in time for the spring dinner plate.
- **Bolt-resistant:** Plants that are not heat tolerant will go to seed when the temperature warms up. This is the plant's desperate way of making babies for next year before it dies. This is problematic, though, when you are not quite done enjoying the tasty vegetable. Once a plant goes to seed, the stems become woody and the taste significantly declines. Arugula becomes too spicy to eat. Broccoli florets become inedible flowers. Selecting varieties for bolt-resistance means they hold out a little longer in the season.
- **Heirloom:** These are plant varieties that were developed over fifty years ago. They were not used in large, commercial agriculture and often have unique characteristics. An heirloom tomato, for example, may have an unusual color or form. Their flavors can often have strong taste characteristics that can add a new layer of depth to cooking. Consider growing an "old and ugly" vegetable-themed garden where you only focus on heirlooms that are warty or unusually shaped. It will add diversity to the plant community and to your palate.
- **Hybrid:** These vegetable varieties are a mixture of two true breeds that have been crossed to produce a hybrid strain. Typically these are high-producing vegetables that can thrive in a wider range of conditions. Sounds perfect, right? The drawback is that the seed cannot be saved and replanted again—it will grow into an unpredictable strain of the plant. Therefore, new seeds must be purchased every year from the seed company. Many of these large seed companies producing hybrids are also actively working on squeezing out organic and heirloom seed companies with the goal of creating a dependent relationship with gardeners who then must buy seed every year from the same company. Not such a great idea.

salvaged materials. Using a hook outside your front door or window, hang the planter, having first filled it with three different kinds of lettuce. I recommend a

You can produce lettuce almost anywhere in a hanging basket.

green leaf lettuce, a red leaf lettuce, and a green butterhead with red speckles. This combination makes an interesting display that is also attractive (and delicious) mixed together in a salad.

Move the ornamental houseplants out and move in an indoor citrus tree. These trees need a sunny place in your apartment that gets direct sun most of the day. They will keep their leaves all year, so it stays pretty inside your apartment, but they work a little harder than the run-of-the-mill rubber tree.

Meyer lemons, kumquats, mandarin oranges, and Kaffir limes are a few of the commonly found indoor citrus plants. Indoor citrus trees are dwarf in size, so they are easy to keep happy in containers. The size of the container will vary based on the size of your tree, but look for the biggest container you can afford and easily move. It will save you the trouble of repotting to a bigger container later on.

Your apartment will smell amazing when these lovely trees are in bloom. Help the blossoms become pollinated by gently swabbing a cotton ball from one flower to another. This exchanges the pollen among all the flowers and increases the fruit production of the tree. These wonderful trees remain mobile, so they can move with you to your next homestead.

PLANTING PLAN: POSTAGE-STAMP PLOT

You need to maximize the size of your garden space by looking for growing opportunities in unconventional places. Make some room in the flower beds for purple kale and rainbow Swiss chard. Their pretty colors blend into an ornamental planting area, and they need only twelve inches of space per plant. They are a cut-and-come-again crop, meaning they keep growing new leaves as you eat the mature ones, creating a long harvest.

Zucchini is an easy-to-grow vegetable that gets about three to four feet high and wide, but delivers a prolific amount of large, juicy squash all season. If you can keep it watered through the summer, you will be rewarded with pounds and pounds of delicious homegrown summer squash. This versatile vegetable is excellent roasted on sandwiches, tossed into pasta, or grated and baked into brownies, cookies, and muffins. You get a lot of harvest bang for the buck.

Beans grow vertically, taking up less garden space.

Squeeze in a container of Asian vegetables on the front porch or parking strip, or tuck it into a corner of the yard. It should include everything you need to make a great stir-fry and still be space efficient. Start with a container about three feet in width, or group several smaller containers together.

Pop in snow pea seeds as soon as the ground can be worked, often around March or April, depending on your planting zone. The snow peas make use of the vertical space by growing up and occupying less surface area. Plant them at the back of the container so they won't shade the other vegetables planted in front of them. Either from seed or nursery-bought starts, arrange Napa cabbage, bok choy, and green onions in the middle and sides of the container. The different colors and textures in the container will look almost too fabulous to eat.

Gather long wooden branches and dig the ends into the ground to make a tipi for beans to climb up and cover. Cherry tomatoes can be trained up the side of a fence using twine as a guide for their vines. Heavier fruiting plants like larger tomatoes and summer squash can also grow vertically on a strong trellis. Create little hammocks for the fruit with used pantyhose, which will support the weight of the fruit so it won't break from the vine as it ripens.

PLANTING PLAN:
THE BACKYARD HOMESTEADER

Even with in-ground garden space, vegetables grown in containers can still be an attractive feature in the yard. Try planting an Italian-themed collection of vegetables in containers or grouped together in a raised bed. They will give you some versatile culinary options over a long growing season, and they share similar watering needs. Choose a quick-ripening ensemble of tomatoes, bell peppers, Italian parsley, green onions, and basil. You can make lots of different pastas and salads using all or just a selection of these great plants.

Tomatoes, the jewels of summer, require careful attention to water. You will also find their flavor increases with the quality of your soil. If you are planting in a container, choose a determinate tomato variety that will only grow to about three feet in height. Indeterminate tomatoes can easily get upward of six feet in height—a good option when you have ample space and want lots of fruit.

When you are working with limited space, pick a tomato variety based on how you plan to use it. Marinara sauce is best made with sauce tomatoes, which have low water content and thick, meaty walls. Sandwiches and burgers are great with a juicy, fat slicer tomato cut into a thick slab. Sweet cherry tomatoes come in a wide range of varieties—classic red, black cherries, little red grape cultivars, yellow pear-shaped ones—and taste great tossed in salads.

Bell peppers and tomatoes both like it hot, so if you live in a milder climate you need to seek out quick-ripening varieties. You will also find the largest selection come from seeds rather than starts. Plan early and think about ways the plants

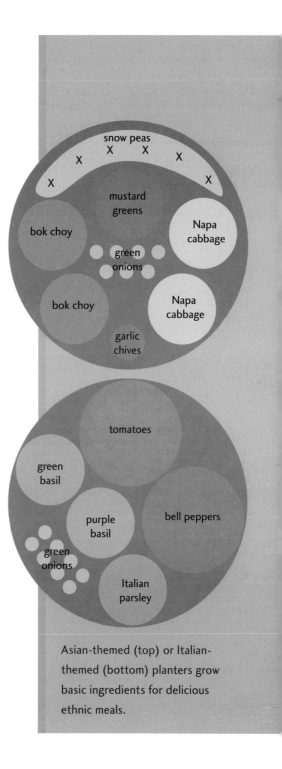

Asian-themed (top) or Italian-themed (bottom) planters grow basic ingredients for delicious ethnic meals.

Help vines trellis upward with garden twine.

can complement each other. Black cherry tomatoes can look great thrown in with yellow sweet peppers in summer salads.

Basil can be a prolific plant if you keep snipping it as it grows. There are a growing number of basil varieties on the market. The traditional Genovese basil varieties look snazzy planted next to dark chocolate or lemony yellow basil plants. Cooking with a mixture of these varieties, or even freezing mixed batches of pesto, adds a wonderful depth of flavor to your dishes.

Green onions take up very little space between these plantings and can often survive colder temperatures, which extends the planting season. Italian parsley needs very little attention to thrive. Both of these plants can also be dried and stored through winter months.

In addition to these and earlier container plantings, pages 58 and 60 show you examples of a rotating planting plan for spring/fall and summer if you have a 10 x 10 foot in-ground plot to work with or a couple of 4 x 8 foot raised beds. It can be difficult to find specific planting plans, because individual site conditions vary so much. Not every plot will have access to full sun, good soil, or be conveniently located in the garden. But it can help to have a starting place that you can modify to fit your light conditions, growing zone, and cooking habits.

This plan includes a crop-rotation schedule so you know what to grow in the colder months and what to transition into the garden when the temperature warms up. Over the course of the growing season, you will have the following vegetable crops:

Beets

Carrots

Lettuce mix: red leaf, green leaf,
  butter leaf, arugula

Swiss chard

Kale

Zucchini

Tomatoes: sauce, slicing, cherry

Broccoli

Peas: snow, snap

Beans: bush, pole

This garden plan has the potential to produce a significant percentage of your produce needs throughout the growing season. In addition to the container plantings, you are on your way to a big harvest. If you're a pretty settled homeowner or a long-term renter, you might want to add some berry bushes and fruit trees in the ground; they typically take longer to get established.

Fruit trees and bushes have traditionally been planted in the backyard, but more and more they are taking over the front yard as well. Don't limit yourself to thinking of them as just edible crops— they are ornamentally valuable plants as well. Cherry blossoms, for example, put on a spectacular show in early spring that can brighten up your whole street.

Often these trees and shrubs need two to three years to develop fruit, so getting started early is key. After we moved into our first house, our neighbor passed on the old saying that the best time to plant a fruit tree is ten years ago. Heeding his advice, I was outside in the fall planting fruit trees and berry bushes before we were even done unpacking. That was perhaps one of the smartest pieces of advice I have received over the years. The anticipation of that first persimmon, fig, and raspberry would have been overwhelming if I had to wait yet another year for fruit.

When placing trees and shrubs in the garden, take into consideration what the plants may shade underneath or behind them. Dwarf fruit trees are often the best choice for home gardens because they rarely exceed ten feet in height, which makes pruning and fruit harvesting much easier. They will still produce an ample harvest for a family to enjoy and even preserve. Those fall leaves also provide something to toss into the compost bin at the end of the season.

PLANTING PLAN COMBINATIONS

From season to season, it can be fun to mix up the combination of vegetables to adhere to a theme. Take your time poring over all those seed catalogs, since every company will have some different varieties. Here are some long lists of fun themes to try:

The Overachiever

This is a great list of plants to work into a garden that is super focused on production. These varieties are quick to mature *and* prolific.

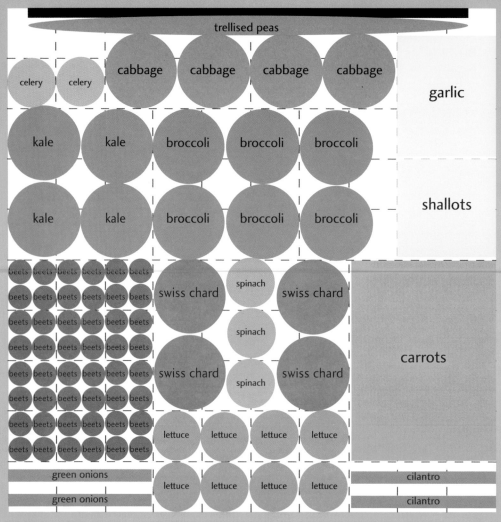

trellised peas

celery · celery · cabbage · cabbage · cabbage · cabbage · garlic

kale · kale · broccoli · broccoli · broccoli · shallots

kale · kale · broccoli · broccoli · broccoli

beets (grid) · swiss chard · spinach · swiss chard · spinach · swiss chard · spinach · swiss chard · carrots

lettuce · lettuce · lettuce · lettuce

green onions · lettuce · lettuce · lettuce · lettuce · cilantro

green onions · cilantro

A cool-weather garden plan can provide a diversity of produce in a small garden space. Depending on your climate zone, this can be a useful option for spring and fall.

Venture bush bean
Kentucky blue pole bean
Pacemaker III beet
Packman broccoli
Red cored Chantenay carrot
Flash collards
Bright lights Swiss chard
Danish ballhead cabbage
Spacemaster cucumber
Millionaire eggplant
Green ice lettuce
Winterbor kale
Sugar baby watermelon
Walla Walla sweet onion
Super sugar snap pea
Northstar bell pepper
Early sweet sugar pie pumpkin
Delicata winter squash
Early butternut squash
Yellow crookneck summer squash
Early girl tomato
Honeybunch cherry tomato

Midnight ruffles lettuce
Russian red kale
Moon and stars watermelon
Red bull onion
Blue podded garden pea
Purple beauty jalapeño pepper
Sweet chocolate pepper
Black futsu squash
Discus bush buttercup winter squash
Mesa queen acorn squash
Dark star zucchini
Black pearl cherry tomato
Paul Robeson tomato

Black and Blue

Deep purples, green-blues, and almost blacks give this garden a unique look. Go for a punky twist by adding edgy garden art like metal bike tires attached to the fence for a trellis.

Royal burgundy bush bean
Purple king pole bean
Bull's blood beet
Purple peacock broccoli
Dragon carrot
Georgia collards
Magenta sunset Swiss chard
Rudy ball cabbage
Black king eggplant

Purple beans add unexpected color to the vegetable garden.

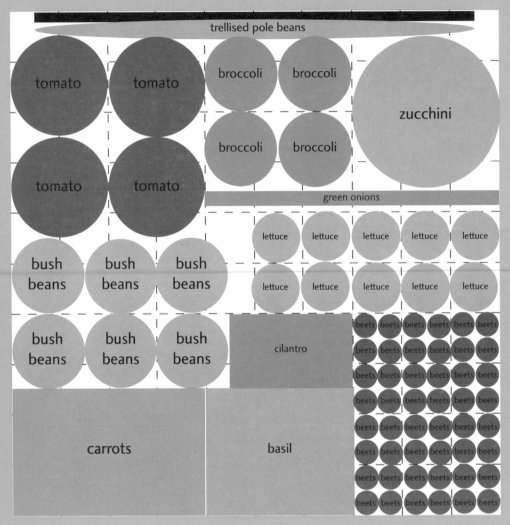

A warm-weather plan will provide multiple options for a long summer harvest.

My favorite heirloom tomato: orange oxheart.

Old and Odd

Unusual heirlooms and quirky new varieties can turn your garden into a funny-shaped, warty planting arrangement.

- Dragon tongue bush bean
- Painted lady runner bean
- Chiogga beet
- Veronica broccoli
- Thumbelina carrot
- Fordhook giant chard
- Lemon cucumber
- Dragon's egg cucumber
- Listada de Gandia eggplant
- Pom pom lettuce
- Forellenschluss lettuce
- Nero di Toscana kale
- Georgia rattlesnake watermelon
- Cipollini onion
- Yellow monster pepper
- Topepo Rosso pepper
- Goosebumps pumpkin
- Rouge Vif D' Etampes pumpkin
- Galeux D'Eysines winter squash
- Marina di Chioggia winter squash
- Bennings green tint scallop squash
- Green zebra tomato
- Pink accordion tomato
- Orange oxheart tomato

Plant Families

Part of the fun of growing your own produce is planning and designing each season's spread. As you get more seasoned, knowing your plant families will help you determine your future garden layouts.

Pests generally become problematic among vegetables that share the same family.

Some gardeners choose to plant vegetables from the same family in the same bed, while others sprinkle them randomly throughout the garden. However you design your growing space, keep track of what was planted where so you can mix it up next season. This allows you to utilize crop rotation, an important design practice for healthy plants.

Some pests will try to overwinter in your soil, so rotating each crop to a new location every season means the bugs have nothing to chew on when they emerge in the spring. Equally important, certain vegetables will deplete soil nutrients faster than others. Kale, for example, is a heavy nitrogen feeder. Moving it to a new location next season gives the soil a chance to build its nitrogen level back up before kale gets planted there again. Try to rotate your garden on a three- or four-year cycle, meaning there are three or four growing seasons before plants get moved back into their original spot.

Here is a list of plant families and their general characteristics:

Brassicas: This family contains more than 350 plant genera, many of which are commonly referred to as cole crops, which like colder weather. They are semihardy and originated from Germany, Great Britain, and southern Europe. These vegetables like colder temperatures and moist soils. They absorb lots of nitrogen, leading to big, green leaves—good since we most often eat the leaves of this family. Plants in this family include broccoli, cabbage, cauliflower, kale, mustard greens, radishes, arugula (or rocket), turnips, brussels sprouts, and collards.

Favaceae: Commonly referred to as the pea or legume family, these plants are nitrogen fixers. Planting them next to or interplanting them with nitrogen-needing vegetables creates a mutually beneficial relationship in the garden. This family of plants originated in the eastern Mediterranean. Popular vegetable crops in this family are peas and beans. Peas can be shelling, snap, or snow varieties. Beans can be either climbing or bush varieties.

Liliaceae: Commonly called the allium or onion family, these produce very pungent-tasting bulbs. Garlic, onions, chives, leeks, and shallots are all part of this family.

Umbelliferae: The common name is the carrot family, which includes plants that have an umbrella-shaped flower. Some of the wild plants in this family are poisonous, so do not attempt to wild forage from this group. Vegetable crops from this family include carrots, parsnips, celery, and fennel. Popular herb varieties include dill, cilantro, parsley, lovage, chervil, and caraway.

Chenopodiacea: Referred to as the beet family, these were originally coastal plants. Popular vegetable crops from this family include beets, spinach, and chard.

Compositae: Sunflower family plants blossom in a cluster of many tiny flowers, forming a larger flower. Common vegetable crops are lettuce, chicory, endive, and dandelions. Sunflowers, artichokes, and thistles are also in this family.

Solanaceae: The nightshade family includes many favorite vegetables along with many wild, poisonous plants. They typically prefer hot climates, originating from tropical and jungle regions. Popular vegetable crops include tomatoes, eggplants, peppers, and potatoes.

Cucurbitaceae: Referred to as the squash family, these are fruiting vines whose seeds can have a long shelf life. Often they respond to cold, wet climates by developing powdery mildew, which weakens the plants' overall health and productivity. Cucumber; summer and winter squashes, including pumpkins; and melons, including watermelons, all belong to this family.

ACQUIRING PLANTS

Preparing a list of what you want to grow this season is an exciting process that also ensures you stick to your gardening budget. I have made many impulse buying decisions at the plant store that have given me some sticker shock. Another smart move is to have your planting areas all prepped before you bring home your new plants or seeds. That allows everything to go into the ground promptly once you get home from the store. If the garden stage has been set, it's time to bring in the players!

There are a lot of options when it comes to acquiring vegetable plants to fill your garden. Growing your plants from seed will give you the widest selection of vegetable varieties. This is more time consuming, as your seedlings will need careful attention to thrive. You will also need a little space to set up the seed trays and grow lights.

You could also opt to buy starts, or small plants, that you can then transplant into the garden. You will not necessarily get the widest selection of varieties with starts, but you will still have a fair selection to choose from. If you are new to gardening, using vegetable starts may be the best option because the plants have been well cared for through the most delicate stage of their young life.

Starting from Seed

Growing your vegetables inside gives you a head start on the growing season, since you can get them nice and mature during the winter months. They will be big and strong by the time you transplant them outside, and that much closer to bearing fruit. For those of us gardening addicts,

Planting from seed offers the widest selection of vegetables.

growing from seed allows us to get our hands dirty before the weather is tolerable.

Seed packets are also a great value, making this a very economical way to grow your crops. A packet of carrot or

lettuce seeds can sometimes have 200 seeds inside! Often there are too many seeds for one homestead to use in a growing season, so consider a seed swap with your gardening buddies.

There are lots of seed companies, so you have lots of options. You could choose to buy from the Seed Savers Exchange, a nonprofit organization committed to saving and sharing heirloom seeds. Or you could choose to support mega-corporations, developers of such things as GMOs, Agent Orange, terminator seeds (ones specifically formulated to not produce viable seed), and numerous highly toxic chemical products.

Many seed companies fall somewhere in between these two extremes. Often I buy from more than one seed company. I might purchase a few packets from Seed Savers Exchange, some rare seeds from a family-owned company, and some impulse packets from my natural grocery store. Take some time to do your research online before you buy. Request catalogs or bookmark company websites so you can choose from the best of the best.

Light and Heat

If you have a warm spot near a south-facing window, it may be possible to grow seeds without a grow light. However, you will get the best results from giving the seedlings access to twelve to sixteen hours of "sunlight" a day. This faux sunlight comes from using a grow light set on a timer. Tricksy!

Grow lights are fairly inexpensive and take up minimal storage space. Start with a small, basic light that provides enough coverage for a couple trays of seedlings. Hang the lights above your seedling area with string or chains that can be adjusted for height. You want the light source about two inches above the seeds. Raise the lights to maintain this distance as they grow upward.

Seedlings in newspaper seed pots.

My indoor living spaces have always been quite small, yet I have always managed to find a nook or cranny to rig up a seed-starting area. Past locations have been on bookshelves, on dresser tops, in closets, on record players, and on the top of the refrigerator. Place an old towel between the surface and the pots if the surface is wooden. Sprinkling water on the seed trays or lightly misting them with water can result in some drips here and there.

The ideal temperature for most vegetable seeds will be somewhere in the neighborhood of 60 to 70 degrees Fahrenheit. Avoid placing seedlings next to a drafty window, where they could get chilled. Some people opt to place a heat mat, sold at garden stores, under the seed trays. This can speed up germination and is a nice extra, but not a necessity. I have personally never used one, and my seedlings have all sprung without them.

Seed-Starting Soil

Your chances of success increase when the quality of the soil increases. You can mix your own seed-starting mix if you plan to use multiple trays for seed starts. There are several recipes out there to choose from, but here is a basic mix:

    3 parts coir
    3 parts vermicompost
    1 part perlite

Coir is organic material produced as a by-product of coconut, made from the husks. It helps with water absorption and retention. Vermicompost provides lots of nutrients for your plants. Perlite lightens the soil for good aeration, allowing oxygen and roots to easily penetrate the soil. All of these ingredients can easily be found in garden shops and nurseries. A bag of each will probably last you more than just one growing season, so split the goods with a friend.

Bags of commercially made seed-starting soil mix are also readily available at garden stores. This is a slightly different mix than regular soil mixes and may be the best option if you are only starting a few trays of seeds. It takes up less space than multiple bags of bulky soil ingredients. Read the label carefully to ensure it contains organic ingredients and does not include peat moss.

Peat should be avoided because it is an unsustainable product. Peat bogs take thousands of years to develop, and peat is often harvested from endangered wetland areas. It is then shipped thousands of miles to outlets where it is sold. On many levels, peat is not an environmentally friendly option.

Seed Pots

A number of things can be used for seed-starting pots, several of which are free. Use your garden cash for the grow light and good soil, not seed pots. Old vegetable-start containers or seed trays from past seasons can be repurposed for seed starting. I save plastic containers from yogurt, butter, and cottage cheese, as well as egg cartons, as winter sets in. Come planting time, I then poke drainage holes in the bottoms and reuse them as seed pots. You can even use old tin cans, provided you make ample drainage holes.

The last few gardening seasons, I have begun to favor old newspapers for seed

Newspaper Seed Pot Steps

1. Take one entire sheet of newspaper and fold vertically. Cut along the horizontal crease so you have two pieces. One piece makes one pot.
2. Fold the newspaper piece over once to make it just a little thicker.
3. Make a roughly $1^1/_2$-inch horizontal fold to act as the lip.
4. Roll the strip of newspaper around a can, leaving about $2^1/_2$ inches overhanging from the bottom of the can.
5. Fold the overhanging $2^1/_2$ inches around the base of the can. This forms the bottom of the pot.
6. Gently slide the paper off the tin can. Press one finger on the bottom of the pot to secure in place while using your other hand to fold over the lip. This secures the pot so it doesn't unravel.
7. Pour in soil. Plant and water as usual.

pots. Tools are sold for wrapping news-paper into pots, but I found a simple method of making them with items lying around the house. The benefit of newspaper seed pots is that the materials are free, easy to assemble, and the starts can be planted right in the ground. The newspaper decomposes, adding mulch into your soil, so the plants have less transplanting shock. Just gently peel back the bottom of the seed pots when planting outside to make it extra easy for the little roots to dig deep into the soil.

Planting Seeds

After setting up your seed-starting area with light and gathering your pots and trays, it is time to sow some seeds. Moisten the soil until it is damp but not soggy. Gently poke in your seeds, following the planting directions on the packets or at a depth of two to three times the seed size. Lightly cover the holes and place under the grow light.

Seeds can take anywhere from a few hours to a few days to germinate, so be patient. A nearby heat source will usually speed up this process. Every morning the anticipation builds as I peek into the seed pots, hoping to spot a new shoot.

As the seedlings grow, they will develop a set of seed leaves, which look different from true leaves. In a few more days, they will develop a larger root system and sprout up their first set of true leaves. These should resemble the leaves of the actual plant. At this point, it's okay to transplant the seedlings to a slightly larger container if necessary. In a few

more weeks, they will be big and strong enough to transition outside.

Check on your seedlings every day and plan to water about every three to five days. Be careful not to overwater the seedlings, which could cause root rot. Consistently wet, soggy soil also contributes to a disease called damping off. The harmful fungus thrives in wet, soggy soil conditions and can kill your plants if allowed to take hold.

As your seeds grow, allow only one plant per pot. If you err on the cautious side and plant two to three seeds per pot, determine the strongest candidate in the pot and pinch out the others. Don't pull the others out of the soil; that can disturb the root system of the selected seedling. Rather, pinch the tops off the less worthy when they are about an inch tall. Throw the pinched-out seedlings onto a salad and enjoy the delicate flavor of the tender sprouts.

Fertilizing Seedlings

Vegetable starts do not need fertilizer for the first couple weeks of growth. After they have one or more sets of true leaves, you can add some diluted fertilizer, being careful not to overdo it. You don't want to burn the plants or shock them with too much of a good thing.

Your plant store can steer you toward many formulas on the market, but I prefer to use diluted fish emulsion. It smells horrible but the seedlings love it, and a little goes a long way. I generally mix two tablespoons into a whole gallon of water, but check the package for their recommendations as well. You may also choose to add a little compost tea to the starts.

Fertilize only every ten to fifteen days. Your plants need time to become good and strong, so don't force them to spring up too aggressively.

Buying Starts

If seed starting is too much for you, opt to buy plant starts that are all ready for transplanting into the garden. You can find plants for sale from a range of different retailers: home improvement stores, grocery stores, garden club sales, farmers' markets, plant shops, and nurseries.

Often the places where plant lovers work will offer you the widest selection and healthiest plants. The top of this list will be plant shops and nurseries—especially local, independently owned ones. They are often slightly more expensive than big-box stores, but they tend to take better care of their plants. Healthier starts mean faster-growing, more-robust plants that will give you bigger harvests.

Farmers' markets and garden club plant sales are equally excellent places to buy plants. They are also a great resource for asking questions or working through garden troubles. Getting to know farmers and gardeners may even result in welcomed

Avoid starts that have become root bound.

friendships with fellow enthusiasts! Farmers' markets and plant sales may not offer as wide a range of plants as the local plant shops, however, and plants are not sold for as long a time period there.

Large home improvement stores or the garden sections of discount retail stores often sell plants in the spring and summer months. Chances are they will be the cheapest option, but you will most

into your shopping cart. Avoid plants that have any brown spots, dead growth, insect eggs, leaf curling, or brown tips. Check the soil they are planted in as well to make sure it is fresh. Green, mossy soil means the plants have been overwatered, so avoid those. Avoid plants that appear root bound from sitting in too small a container for too long. They will never make healthy plants.

Be gentle as you transplant your vegetable starts—we all hate moving!

likely have a selection limited to the most popular vegetables and hybrid varieties. There are exceptions, but generally these stores will not have the highest-quality plants. Bigger plants sell better, making it likely they were overpumped with fertilizers.

Carefully look over plant starts for pests and disease before they make it

Don't be afraid to be the person carefully looking through each pot for the best, healthiest plants. I have no shame anymore about poking around in the container before buying, because I have brought home too many plants over the years that turned out to be root bound. Careful selection now increases your potential for success in the garden.

We can all agree that moving to a new home is stressful and a total drag. Transplanting seedlings makes them feel just as agitated. You can minimize their trauma by being gentle with them during planting.

Begin by acclimating the starts to the outdoor environment, a process called hardening off. About a week prior to their recommended planting date, check the forecast to make sure there is good, even weather ahead—no hot spells and no cold snaps. Water them a little less and take a hiatus from fertilizing. Bring the seedlings outside to a sheltered spot of the garden for a few hours every day. At night, bring them back inside. Do this for about a week, gradually leaving them out longer and in sunnier locations. After the week is up, they should be acclimated to their new outdoor world. It's time to transplant.

Dig a hole larger than your plant when you are ready to transplant. Gently lift the plant out by its leaves, not its stem. If you accidentally squeeze it too tight, the leaves can regrow. Crushing the stems, though, is bad, bad news. It can be helpful to squeeze the pot to loosen the plant from the container walls. Loosen the soil around the roots and nestle the plant into the hole you have dug. Gently pull soil around the plant and pat down. Water the newly transplanted start well. Keep a close eye on it for the next several days, watering often until it gets established.

PLANT WATERING

Vegetables prefer deep watering, so opt to water them well every three to five days as opposed to a light sprinkling every day. Plants from smaller seeds, like carrots and lettuces, may need a more frequent, light watering to get established. The frequency of watering may need to increase when the temperature rises above 90 degrees Fahrenheit. Check the dryness of the soil by sticking your finger down a couple inches. If it feels sandy and dry, it's time to water. If there is some dampness, they can go a little longer.

Containers dry out faster than in-ground gardens, so be prepared to check on your pretty pots regularly. When the soil feels dry, I water them until water begins trickling out from the bottom drainage holes. This tells me that the soil is sufficiently moistened. The pots will feel heavy when you lift them if there is moisture in there, and light when they are too dry.

Plants have their own language we need to learn to understand. They tell you when they are thirsty with drooping leaves and pale coloration. Avoid letting them get to this point by checking on your little friends each morning or evening. Yellowing leaves tell you they are not getting enough nutrients from the soil. Consider fertilizing them to encourage growth.

Water in the morning or evening to allow the water time to sink into the soil and around the plant roots, otherwise it may evaporate off the surface too quickly from the afternoon sun. This may seem like a hassle at first when you consider how hard it is already to get to work on time every morning, but building it into your routine has its rewards. I look forward to my mornings of sipping coffee and visiting my plants before heading off to work. It is a wonderful way to get centered before the day begins.

PESTS AND DISEASE: SPOTTING PROBLEMS, PREVENTION, DECLARING WAR

After all your loving care planting your garden, you will spend the next few months tending to your empire. An old Chinese proverb says "The best fertilizer is the gardener's shadow," which holds true. Minding your garden every day means you will notice subtle changes and hints of problems before they turn into catastrophes.

Pests are often specific to certain plant families, which is another reason why a solid planting plan will help you in the long run. If a pesky bug starts wreaking havoc on your cabbage, any nearby broccoli will likely suffer from the same fate, as they are both in the *Brassica* family. See the list in this section on pages 62–63 for details on vegetable families, and plant members of families in separate areas. It will be harder for pests to ruin an entire family of vegetables if they have to travel a longer distance to get to them all.

Practicing annual crop rotation can help decrease the probability of pests. Crop rotation means you plant tomatoes

Leaf miner, a common pest, lives in the leaves of beets and Swiss chard.

Spray aphids with diluted dishwashing soap.

The dish soap will dry out their bodies, and they will fry. Once the bugs are dead, hose off the plant with a strong spray to remove the leftover carnage and wash off the soapy water, which can also irritate the plant over time.

Slugs can also be problematic in the garden. There are several organic remedies on the market, like Sluggo, that can be safe for pets if accidentally ingested. You can also bury a half-filled container of beer into the ground. The slugs will be attracted to the beer, fall in, and drown. Placing a plank of wood on the path near the affected plants will draw the slugs underneath during the day. You can then flip the board over and do away with them.

Because there is a wide range of potential pests and they vary based on your region, get friendly with your local plant shop or extension office. Often you can bring in a snipping of an affected plant and they can guide you to a remedy. Just keep in mind that whatever you use in your garden will eventually end up in our water system, so choose nontoxic and organic whenever possible.

in a different place this year than you did last year. Ideally, you do this in a three-year cycle, where plants get a new spot every year until they return to their original location after the third year. Pesky insects lay larvae in the soil to hatch in spring. Pests will get an early hold and become a big problem when the same plant affected by the pest last summer is in the same spot in spring.

An easy, nontoxic homemade spray can be applied to your plants if unwanted bugs begin to take hold. Mix a teaspoon of nontoxic dishwashing soap with two cups water in a spray bottle. Spray the soft-bodied insects until well soaked.

Beneficial Insects

Before you start running outside to spray every bug you see with diluted dishwashing soap, know that not all bugs are bad. In fact, one of your best defenses against unwanted bad bugs is to have a garden full of good bugs.

Good bugs include ladybugs, lacewings, spiders, and ground beetles. Their diet consists of the bad guys: aphids,

Beneficial insects such as bees are a garden friend.

root maggots, slug eggs, and so on. They supplement their meal with the nectar of various flowering plants.

Flowers are beautiful in the garden, but before you make room for them think about those that serve double duty. Here is a short list (there are far more to choose from) of some of my favorite garden flowers that are both pretty to look at and attract beneficial insects:

Sunflower
Jerusalem artichoke
Zinnia
Marigold
Mustard green
Alyssum
Cilantro

Dill
Lovage
Fennel
Sea holly
Angelica
Buckwheat
Pea

In addition to adding these flowers, think about where the good bugs can overwinter in the garden. They typically want a dense, evergreen spot near the garden where they can escape the cold winter and resurface in the spring. Evergreen trees, shrubs, and ground covers, including herbs, are a welcome home for them and encourage them back into the garden early next season.

Keeping Notes

There is an old musing that "no garden is as great as next year's garden." The surest way to learn from your mistakes is to keep track of them.

I keep a notebook in my garden tool area; in it I write down little notes from the day. I write the date and things like "Snow peas blooming"; "Tomato end rot on romas"; or "Aphids attacking the broccoli." Then for the next year I can refer to this book to learn the patterns of when certain pests seem to attack or how quickly something germinated in a semishady spot. It only takes a minute to write that you overplanted zucchini but wish you had more soybeans.

A garden journal also helps to plan crop-rotation schedules. You may not recall if that was last year or the year before that the kale and collard greens were planted in the containers closest to the back door. Make it easy on yourself by keeping track of what gets planted where and when.

Your garden journal serves a larger purpose than simply being a collection of gardening notes. We plant more than just seeds in a well-loved garden. The journal holds memories of sunny days, swelling storms, fragrant blossoms, defeat and triumph. You may find it becomes a sentimental keepsake of your journey.

Good Night, Garden

Although I can safely describe myself as a gardening junkie, it never fails that fall rolls in and I feel ready to throw in the towel. Perhaps I can muster some motivation to plant overwintering crops like leeks, garlic, and cabbage before it gets bitterly cold outside, but generally I enjoy taking a couple months off and enjoying the fruits of my labor.

As your garden season comes to a close, take the time to clean up the stray pots, hoses, and loose bags of soil. They need to be protected from the winter weather in cool, dry storage places. Rake

A garden journal will help you learn from previous mistakes.

the leaves and keep them near your compost pile, or spread them directly onto your planting beds so they can compost in place.

Enjoy these last few weeks of the growing season by meandering through the garden or pausing by your windowsills or planters to harvest your plants often. You never know when an early frost will hit unexpectedly and you'll lose those last tomatoes prematurely. Look out on the empire you set out to build back in the spring and take note of just how far you have come.

It's this time of year that I start retreating from the garden and into the kitchen. All of that delicious, homegrown produce needs to be preserved to get us through the cold winter months. I start to busily plan get-togethers with friends to swap produce and strategize what gets made into food gifts for the holidays.

A homesteading life changes with each season as a new list of projects and plans replaces those from the previous season. Mash the last of the fresh raspberries onto some crusty toast, grab a mug of tea, and say good-bye to the growing season.

Chapter Three
CITIFIED CRITTERS

Travel around most urban areas in the world and you'll be surprised to see which feathered or furry critters are living there. There may not be quite as many dogs or cats, but chickens on balconies or ducks scurrying around a small shaded patio are not uncommon sights. The noise of buzzing mopeds and humming delivery trucks mixes with the baaing of milk goats. What we think of as farm animals can actually fit in well to our urban spaces—and they work hard to earn their keep.

It used to be much more common to keep urban livestock than it is today. My mother initially thought my idea of keeping backyard chickens sounded bonkers, but my grandparents thought it was quite practical. In fact, my little ninety-six-year-old nana told me stories of living in Portland, Oregon, back in the 1930s and selling chicken eggs from their backyard flock to get them through the Great Depression. Ask your own grandparents, and they may recall stories of growing up with a flock of chickens in the neighborhood, or even in their family's

Bantam chickens take very little space in the city.

backyard. Some of them haven't told those stories for decades, and they can be a great resource as your homestead starts clucking.

The tide began to turn on urban livestock somewhere around midcentury. The animals headed for the hills—or countryside—and industrialized food became the new fashion. Small family farms started to fade, and big factories sprang up. All the milk, eggs, and meat a family could need was available for low prices at emerging megastores known as supermarkets.

Those large commercial food factories that once seemed like such a perfect solution to the nation's food problems are now falling off their pedestal. Reports on food safety and animal cruelty, which are released on a regular basis, should certainly make us think a little more about our steak dinners. I think about things we used to take for granted, like whether the meat before me was an organically fed animal, pumped with hormones, or injected with antibiotics. I was just planning on eating dinner, not chemicals.

Raising our own urban livestock, whether it's for eggs, meat, or milk, gives us peace of mind about what kind of lives these animals have lived. We know what injections they have or have not had. We can make sure they are eating high-quality food and living high-quality lives out in the sunshine and fresh air, as nature intended.

Keeping animals in the city requires a higher level of responsibility, but also delivers some serious rewards. A small backyard flock of chickens does not require

Finch House

My grandpa Egger was an accomplished woodworker and an avid gardener who always had the tidiest rows of vegetables. For years he made several sharp-looking yet simple birdhouses that were the perfect places for finches to nest in the early spring. Native birds have such a way of bringing life into the smallest urban corners, and I will always appreciate him for introducing me to them.

The houses can be made from a wide range of found or salvaged materials. Finches are especially common birds throughout the United States, so no matter where you live they can have a place to call home.

Materials

- Two $3/4$-inch-thick pieces of redwood or cedar cut to $5^1/_2$ x 6 inches
- Three $3/4$-inch-thick pieces of redwood or cedar cut to 6 x 6 inches
- One $3/4$-inch-thick piece of redwood or cedar cut to 6 x 7 inches
- Box of $5/8$-inch wood screws
- Two $3/4$-inch metal hinges and one 1-inch eyehole and one latch

1. Use naturally rot-resistant wood, preferably cedar or redwood. Do not paint the wood.
2. Drill four $1/4$-inch holes in one of the 6 x 6-inch pieces, one in each corner. This will be used as the floor of the birdhouse. The holes provide drainage.
3. Drill a $1^1/_2$-inch hole into the middle of another piece of 6 x 6-inch wood. This will act as the front of the birdhouse.
4. Screw the front of the birdhouse into the two $5^1/_2$ x 6-inch pieces, which will be the sides of the house. The bottoms should be flush, which will create a $1/2$-inch ventilation gap at the top of the walls.
5. Screw the back of the birdhouse into place, using the remaining 6 x 6-inch piece.
6. Screw the bottom of the birdhouse into each wall. This is the 6 x 6-inch piece that has drainage holes in the corners.
7. Arrange the 6 x 7-inch piece into place as the roof of the birdhouse. It should overhang the front entrance by 1 inch. Screw the two hinges into the roof piece and connect them to the back wall. Assemble the eyehole and latch to a side wall for security.
8. Situate the finch house on a fence post in a semiexposed area. Placing it next to trees or shrubs could allow predators to enter the house.
9. In the fall, unlatch the rooftop piece to clean out debris from the house.

Chickens can be both a beautiful and a productive addition to the urban homestead.

a tremendous amount of maintenance, and you will be collecting homegrown eggs most months of the year. Goats are a much more serious commitment of time and energy, with milking responsibilities twice a day, but you will also be able to put healthy milk on the table each night and still have enough leftovers for a batch of tangy goat cheese.

Urban livestock give an extra kickback to the garden in the form of nitrogen-rich manure. Turn it into the compost pile and watch how your garden thanks you with produce when the humus gets turned into the soil. Just like with other homemade goods, I have traded excess chicken manure from my girls, in this case for tulip bulbs from a neighbor. She

enjoyed the fertilizer and I got to enjoy more flowers. The deeper into homesteading you get, the more alternative forms of currency you discover.

For those not wishing to jump into the raising scene, there are other enticing ideas and projects for you and your interests in this chapter—creating habitat for local birds and other wildlife. You may be surprised to learn that even the smallest of spaces can still offer you several options for a self-reliant homestead. Homesteads have a way of growing over time, and there are many backyard livestock options to choose from. Soon you will be spending less time watching the TV and more time watching the animal channel outside your window.

THE LOCALS

As cities expand, habitat for native birds and bees declines. But there are ways for us to carve out more hospitable nooks and crannies for our feathered and buzzing friends. The following projects can be made with minimal supplies and put to good use at any homestead—from a massive estate to a studio apartment.

HOT CHICKS

Keeping a flock of backyard chickens may seem a little strange at first, but once you start you'll kick yourself for not moving your flock in sooner. You'll quickly realize how low-maintenance, friendly, and entertaining a flock of chickens can be.

Americans are rekindling their love affair with raising backyard birds, and many urban areas already allow small flocks without any added legwork. Some cities have a permitting process that can range from a simple form to several hoops to jump through. The best way to find out what is considered legal in your area is to contact your local extension office or call the city. Homeowners' associations may have their own restrictions as well.

Chickens 101

Chickens are fairly quiet birds that require minimal maintenance and in turn provide delicious eggs, nitrogen-rich manure, and endless entertainment. Their life span can vary wildly, but seven to ten years is a good average to plan on.

The word *hen* refers to a female chicken, and *rooster* applies to the males. A common misconception is that you need a rooster for a hen to lay an egg, which is not the case. Hens regularly lay unfertilized eggs without a rooster—those are the eggs you buy at the grocery store. If they do the wild thing with a rooster, they lay fertilized eggs. You can still eat these eggs, but if the hen decides to sit on them for a month, they will eventually hatch into little chickies.

Although most cities in the United States allow a small backyard flock of hens, they generally prohibit roosters due to their noise, since they don't just crow in the morning. (Now if only we could get our cities to prohibit dogs that bark all night, excessive honking, and rowdy neighbors.) For the purpose of egg production, a small group of hens is all you need.

There are two categories of chickens based on size: standards and bantams. Standard chickens are full size and lay the eggs that we are used to seeing on grocery store shelves. Bantams are miniature chickens that are roughly a fifth to half the size of a standard chicken. They take up less living space and lay small eggs about half the size of a standard hen. Did I mention they are adorable?

Chickens can live happily in a well-built coop, but they will really enjoy free-ranging in the backyard. In the open there is more for them to forage on than just regular chicken feed, and they find it very exciting. The bugs, worms, grass, and other plant material they eat will also make their eggs taste richer and the yolks even darker in color.

My girls have quickly learned how delicious a fresh tomato tastes and will

Bee House

Native bees are solitary creatures, meaning they live on their own rather than with a colony in a hive. These native bees need places to hole up for the winter months. Typically they do this in dense, undisturbed evergreen vegetation, but that can be hard to find in the city. As bee populations continue to fluctuate widely, building a place for them to overwinter will help their survival rate and also increase pollination.

Another simple project I learned from my grandpa is this native bee house that you can hang almost anywhere. Although I started with just one, I now have several bee houses on fence posts in the backyard and near the windows of my house. It is exciting to watch the holes fill up through the winter, with the bees emerging in the spring.

Materials

- One 2 x 4 cedar or redwood board, cut to 6 inches
- One eyehole hook

1. Use untreated, naturally rot-resistant wood like cedar or redwood and leave unpainted.
2. Drill a variety of hole sizes from $1/2$ inch, $3/8$ inch, $1/4$ inch, and $3/16$ inch in width on one side of the wood. Drill roughly three $3/4$-inch holes into the 4-inch-thick piece of wood. Different bee species prefer different sizes, so this gives them some options. Space the holes about $1/2$ inch apart from each other.
3. Screw the eyehole hook into the top of the box. Hammer a long nail into a fence post or exterior wall, then hang box from hook.
4. Hang roughly 4 feet above ground facing south, avoid strong wind areas.

make a beeline right for the vegetable garden to wreak havoc. Having a separate fence around your vegetable beds is ideal, but I have never enjoyed that setup. Instead, I let them have total free range of the garden in the winter months. They work the soil in the vegetable beds for me by directly adding nitrogen-rich manure and tilling it into the soil as they hunt for bugs. To prevent garden carnage the rest of the year, I cover my vegetable beds with irrigation hoops and tie bird netting over the hoops. Pollinators can still visit the flowering plants, but the chickens can't have access to my prized produce.

Your flock will still be happy if they can't free range. Give them more kitchen scraps to keep their diet varied and treat them hand-picked bugs if their coop is not on a dirt floor. If you have a small patio or balcony, a small flock of chickens may be a good option for you. And if you're a renter, just clear it with the landlord first.

Making Peace

Before you hammer a single nail into your future coop or run out to buy some baby chicks, take the first steps toward being a responsible pet owner: check the laws and requirements in your area, and talk to your landlord (if applicable) and your neighbors about your clucking endeavors. Even if keeping chickens in your area does not require any consent from the neighbors, establishing good relations and a clear line of communication ensures you are working toward a stronger community. You want to avoid

any neighbor complaints of noise or nuisance, which could make it harder for chickens to stay in the city. You will want to cover a few hot topics of interest with them: legality, smell, and noise.

Many people may not know whether it is legal or not to keep chickens in the city, so explain your local code so they understand nothing illegal is going on in your backyard. Let them rest assured that you plan on changing their coop bedding regularly, so they should not be experiencing any barnyard smells coming from

Maude, my Brahma hen, enjoys some sunshine in the city.

your backyard. And finally, explain that you do not have any plans for a rooster that will crow all day and night.

Chickens, especially those breeds suitable for urban areas, are docile creatures and fairly quiet animals. You may hear soft clucking, and occasionally the girls may squawk at the excitement of laying a new egg, but aside from those few minutes of the day, your neighbors will most likely not notice the birds among the hum of other city noises.

It is important that your neighbors know they can come to you with any questions or concerns after the birds arrive. A little bribing with some organic, homegrown eggs certainly helps smooth things over with the reluctant folks. Or perhaps bring them cookies that were made with your backyard eggs. Just like gardening, keeping chickens is a great way to strengthen ties with neighbors and keep your local community strong.

Housing

Chicken coops are typically divided into two areas: the henhouse and the run. The whole structure is referred to as the coop. Coops range from rustic flophouses to architecturally sophisticated chicken estates. Your flock could happily live in an altered wooden box with an opening leading to a ramshackle fenced area. They could also live it up in a professionally crafted minihouse built to replicate your own, complete with insulation, electricity, and a heating unit.

I tend to favor old apartments and old houses, most of which have no side insulation. Therefore I can't bring myself to build a coop that is more insulated than my own house, so generally my coops are more than a shack, but far from an estate. Most chicken coops end up somewhere between these two extremes as well.

The henhouse is the part of your chicken coop where your chickens sleep and lay eggs. Whatever clever and creative design you end up using for your henhouse, it is important that the structure stays dry, provides shelter from the sun and wind, allows for good ventilation, and protects against predators.

Wet conditions encourage bacteria growth, which can lead to disease problems in your flock. Make sure doors open and shut snuggly, there are no holes in the roofing, and the henhouse is situated in a place with good drainage. Rainwater should drain away from the site of your henhouse.

Chickens like temperatures that range from 45 to 80 degrees Fahrenheit. When the weather gets hot, they need a place to hide from the sun. When things get chilly, the henhouse needs to protect them from cold drafts. You do not need to insulate your henhouse if you live in a mild climate. Do plan to insulate your coop if you live in an area with cold winters or hot summers. Materials like old packing peanuts, Styrofoam, old jeans cut up into scraps, and newspaper can be good low-cost insulation options. Sandwich this between two sheets of plywood to keep the chickens from pecking it apart.

Good ventilation helps your coop cool down during the hot summer months.

Florence, a Rhode Island Red, announces her freshly laid eggs.

trees out in the wild and on roosts in chicken coops. Your henhouse should have roosts placed eighteen to twenty-four inches or more above the floor for sleeping. Often the higher roosts become the preferred sleeping spot. If you have multiple roosts, stagger their position so no one gets pooped on! Allow about twelve inches of space per bird on the roost.

Roosts are best when they are slightly rounded so the chickens can wrap their feet around them for stability. Wood is king, as smoother textures can be hard for the chickens to grip. Closet dowels make good, practical chicken roosts, but try to scout out the perfect tree branch instead. Adding a natural touch here and there can really make your coop the hip addition to the backyard.

Chickens prefer laying their eggs in dark, dry, private places. Providing a roughly 12 x 12-inch box open on one side allows them a clean and comfortable spot for egg laying. Use straw or pine shavings to line the floor. Plan to have one nesting box per four chickens, which they will take turns using.

With my flock of only three chickens, I was worried about a queue for the nesting box. It reminded me of having three teenage girls all fighting to use the bathroom at the same time. I decided to build them a second nesting box so no one had to wait. Three eggs would always be in the same nesting box, which confused me. When I moved an egg into the other nesting box, they only laid in the new place. When I moved an egg back to the original nesting box, they only laid in the original spot.

The air circulation also brings in fresh oxygen for your birds and blows out the harmful gasses they create from defecating. Allow for ventilation by cutting large holes along the top of the henhouse sides. You can also cut and hinge small openings along the henhouse sides that can be left open in summer and closed in winter. Depending on the size of your ventilation areas, you may need to line the back of them with wire to prevent the chickens from using them as doors.

Chickens instinctively sleep above the ground for protection from predators—in

It took me a couple weeks of this routine to realize that chickens prefer adding their egg to a place where someone else already laid an egg. They are always on a quest to gather enough eggs to sit on and hatch, so the second nesting box for only three hens proved useless. Sorry, girls, I guess you'll have to queue after all for your turn in the ladies' room.

As they begin to lay eggs, place a fake egg, which you can buy at your feed store, in the nesting box. This will help train your girls where to lay their eggs. It's really not fun to have an Easter egg hunt every evening, so do not let them start laying eggs in random places. In fact, if you plan to let your girls free range, hold off until they have been laying for a week or two. It's hard to break the habit if they decide to start laying eggs under your porch steps or behind a thick shrub.

Construct the henhouse for easy cleaning and egg collection. A hinged door on one side allows you to swing the henhouse open to rake out used bedding. It also makes egg collection very simple. I prefer my coops to sport two doors on their henhouses: one that swings fully open for cleaning and a minidoor next to the nesting box for egg collection.

Chicken runs can be uncovered, but I highly recommend your run be covered. This protects your flock from determined raccoons or hawks attempting to feast on a fresh chicken dinner. It also provides shade during hot days and shelter from rain and snow. Covered runs tend to keep some heat in the space, even if the sides are built with fencing. Many

winter mornings I have seen snow covering everything outside except the area in and around the chicken coop.

Chicken runs are typically made of chicken wire or wire mesh called hard cloth. Hard cloth tends to be a little more expensive, but it is also stronger—making it more difficult for a raccoon or loose dog to pull off. Many runs have a hinged door or removable side that allows for easy cleaning and access to the food and water dispensers. A run that is six feet high can comfortably fit a person standing inside. Alternatively, a four-foot-high run takes up less physical and visual space in the garden.

Ready-built coops are becoming increasingly available through online classified ads, local carpenters, and national coop companies like Eglu. You may have some luck looking for second-hand coops in your local paper or online classified listings. Consider altering an already-built structure to suit your needs.

The classic wooden doghouse, for example, could easily be modified for chicken living. Build a run around the doghouse and add legs on the bottom of the house to raise it above the ground. Convert one side of the doghouse into a door by adding a hinge, add a removable nesting box, and place a roost inside. *Eh voilà*: doghouse becomes chicken pad!

Building a chicken coop should be a rewarding experience only limited by your imagination. Often this can be an overwhelming idea for beginners, and it's difficult to know where to begin. I had never done more than hammer a nail into a wall to hang a picture before I built my first chicken coop. It did not go down in history as the world's prettiest coop, but the chickens seemed to like it just fine. Even a complete novice can build a sturdy and functional coop.

Start by carefully planning out the details of your coop prior to purchasing your materials. Sketch it out, make a list of all the cuts you will need, and think through the order in which you'll assemble things. Try hard not to get too frustrated when boards don't line up perfectly or something looks a little crooked. Remind yourself that this is a house for chickens and they are not picky! Two heads are better then one, so try to enlist a friend to help out. Although it can be done on your own, it's a lot easier to do things like hinge a door with two people.

To get you started, I offer you two chicken coop plans practical for a small flock of three hens. The first coop plan (pages 91–95) is built for three standard hens and includes storage for all of your supplies: bedding, feed, oyster shell, grit, etc. It is also portable! If you decide to move, portability makes things much easier so the girls can move with you. The henhouse detaches from the run so each unit can be lifted easily by two people.

The second chicken coop (pages 96–98) is a minicoop for some minihens: bantams. If you are limited to a small balcony or patio, you can still have chickens. Bantams need half the coop space of standard chickens and will delight you with mini-eggs that are just as tasty as the big girls'. A terrific feature of this coop is the attached worm bin, so you can do your composting in the same spot you raise your chickens. When you clean out the coop, the manure-filled straw goes straight into the worm bin, providing the browns you need for making compost.

Standard Chicken Coop

This design is intended to fit into space-challenged areas and comfortably house three standard-sized hens. Have the materials cut to size by the lumber store if you want to skip sawing the pieces yourself. The coop features a base storage area for bedding and feed, a cupboard for additional supplies, a henhouse, and

The minicoop comfortably houses three bantam hens. A worm bin sits on the top left.

a chicken run. The run can be separated from the henhouse/storage area when it needs to move. You could even add wheels to the bottom of the henhouse/storage area for even easier moving.

Supplies

If you are new to keeping chickens, plan on feeding your flock chicken feed in the form of pellets or crumbles from your local pet or feed store. You will need to buy chicken feed specifically for layers, which is what your flock will be. This feed ensures they have the proper mix of nutrients to support laying eggs. Advanced chickenkeepers may choose to mix their own chicken feed rather than buying it commercially prepared, but leave this for the well-seasoned chicken farmers.

Almost every feed store will give you the option of organic layer feed. Chicken feed is often sold in large, fifty-pound bags, so don't expect to carry it home in your arms. Bring the geezer cart if you are taking public transportation so you can wheel it home, or be prepared to carry the large load a short distance to your car or a taxi.

Feed stores also sell chicken feeders that you can hang on a hook inside the run. There is a rimmed plate at the bottom with a cylinder attached to it. The feed goes into the cylinder, which holds multiple days' worth of feed at a time. Feed continues to slide down as the chickens eat from the plate.

Plan to feed your flock some scratch in addition to chicken feed. Scratch is a mixture of dried corn and grains. Think of scratch as a dessert item—the chickens will love it, which helps get them used to being near people, but eating too much will lead to fat chickens. I throw some scratch into the run of my coop to entice the girls to turn their bedding looking for the morsels, keeping the bedding light and clean. I may feed them a bit more as winter approaches to get them slightly chunkier for when cold weather comes in. It also gives them more energy, which they will need in the winter to stay warm. Scratch is readily available at feed stores or wherever chicken feed is sold.

Eggshells contain large amounts of calcium, so providing your girls with access to a calcium source is recommended. This commonly comes in the way of oyster shell, which is broken down into little flakes and sold at feed stores. Some people mash up used eggshells and let their chickens eat that instead. There is something a little gross to me, though, about feeding an animal something that actually came out of its body at some point. I'll let you decide for yourself on that one.

Put a small container of the calcium supplement in the run and the chickens will regulate things themselves, eating it when they feel they need it. I find an old tuna can hammered about eight inches off the ground works well. If you do not provide them with additional calcium, the result will be thin-shelled eggs that can possibly break when laid. Chickens have been known to eat their eggs, which can be a difficult habit to break. Don't give them any tasting opportunities with weak-shelled eggs.

Constructing the Chicken Run

Materials

- Thirteen 2 x 4s, 48 inches long
- Two 2 x 2s, 40½ inches long
- Two 2 x 2s, 14 inches long
- One-pound box wood screws
- Four L-shaped brackets
- 48-inch-tall wire mesh
- Poultry staples
- Two metal hinges and one latch

1. Arrange four 2 x 4s to create a square and screw together. Repeat.
2. Attach these two squares together using a 2 x 4 in each corner of the squares, which will make a box.
3. Position the last 2 x 4 close to one of the corners to create a 17-inch opening, which will be where the door to the run is hung.
4. Hammer in wire mesh with poultry staples. Leave an opening where the door will be. Leave one side of the run open. This is where the run will attach to the henhouse and storage area.
5. Construct the door out of the 2 x 2s using the metal L-shaped brackets, one for each corner of the rectangle. Screwing the pieces directly into one another may split the wood, so use the brackets to screw them together.
6. Hammer wire mesh over the door with poultry staples.
7. With the help of a friend, use two hinges to hang the door to the frame of the coop and position the latch into place.

Chickens do not have teeth and instead rely on small rocks they keep in their gizzard to grind up food particles. When food is eaten, it is held in the gizzard, where it is rubbed together with these little rocks until it's broken down enough to move on to the stomach. These small bits of rock are referred to as grit. You should make grit available to your flock. Chickens will naturally pick up grit material in the soil when allowed to free range, but it's not a bad idea to provide some in another little tuna can in the run. They will eat it when their body needs it.

Like all animals, chickens need constant access to clean, cool water. It is quite possible for them to die by going only a few hours without water on a severely hot day. You can find water dispensers at the feed store. If you live in a warm or hot climate, it may be wise to invest in a larger size to ensure they will not run out of water on a hot summer day. Like the other supplies, keep the water dispenser raised off the ground, at breast level. This keeps straw and other muck from getting into the water. Use a stable platform, like a cinder block, to prevent your chickens from tipping over their water as they scratch around the coop.

Choosing Breeds

When I talk about my favorite chicken breeds, most people respond with "There are breeds of chickens?" The answer is yes, several. Although not all are perfect for urban flocks, there are at least a dozen to choose from that should work for you. This is yet another fun part of urban chickenkeeping.

Backyard breeds tend to be quieter, less skittish, and steady layers. They are also less likely to go broody, which means they stubbornly sit on the eggs waiting for them to hatch for weeks at a time. A broody hen needs to be forced off the egg pile and quarantined for a few days to break her of the intention to hatch babies. She will stop laying eggs during this time until the broodiness passes.

Here is a list of chicken options commonly found at feed stores and through catalog order:

Ancona
Andalusian
Araucana/American (blue-green eggs)
Australorp
Barred Rock
Brahma (feathered feet)
Buff Orpington
Jersey Giant
Leghorn
New Hampshire Red
Polish (little fluffy balls on their heads)
Rhode Island Red
Wyandottes

White leghorn Brahmas are similar in appearance to standard leghorns, just smaller.

Constructing the Storage Base

Materials

- Two 2 x 2s, 20 inches long
- Two 2 x 2s, 21 inches long
- Four 2 x 2s, 48 inches long
- Two $^1/_2$-inch-thick plywood pieces cut to 2 x 2 feet
- Two $^1/_2$-inch-thick plywood pieces, cut to 2 x 4 feet
- Two metal hinges and one latch
- One-pound box wood screws

1. Arrange the 2 x 2s to make a rectangular frame that is a 2 x 2 x 4-foot box and screw together. This becomes the base of the coop, which the storage cupboard and henhouse will sit on.
2. Screw the 2 x 4-foot plywood pieces onto opposite sides of the box to make the top and bottom of the storage base.
3. On one end of the box, screw one of the 2 x 2-foot plywood pieces into the frame.
4. With the help of a friend, use the remaining 2 x 2-foot plywood piece to make a door into the storage base. Use two hinges to attach it to the frame of the storage base and position the latch into place.

Constructing the Storage Cupboard Frame

Materials

- Four 2 x 2s, 21 inches long
- Four 2 x 2s, 11$^1/_2$ inches long
- Wood screws left over from base

1. Arrange the 2 x 2s together to make a tall, narrow box and screw together. This will be the frame of the storage cupboard.

Basic carpentry skills are helpful, but the chickens won't mind if things are not perfectly aligned.

Constructing the Henhouse Frame

Materials

- Four 2 x 2s, 36 inches long
- Four 2 x 2s, 21 inches long
- Four 2 x 2s, 32$\frac{1}{2}$ inches long
- Wood screws left over from base

1. Screw the 2 x 2s together to make a box that is 36 x 36 x 24 inches in size. This will be the frame of the henhouse.

Assembling the Standard Chick Coop

Materials

- Two $\frac{1}{2}$-inch thick plywood pieces, 48 x 60 inches
- One $\frac{1}{2}$-inch thick plywood piece, 24 x 36 inches
- Two $\frac{1}{2}$-inch-thick plywood pieces, 36 x 25 inches
- Wood screws left over from base
- Corrugated metal roofing, 52 x 26$\frac{1}{2}$ inches
- Four metal hinges and two latches

1. Place the storage base into position. Place the henhouse frame onto one side of the storage base, leaving $\frac{1}{2}$ inch of space from the edges of the base. Screw the frame into the storage base.
2. Screw the 24 x 36-inch plywood piece onto one side of the storage cupboard.
3. Place the storage cupboard of the other side of the storage base, with the plywood wall against the frame of the henhouse. Screw into the storage base.
4. Screw the frame of the henhouse into the shared wall of the storage cupboard.
5. Cut a 12 x 12-inch opening into one of the large 48 x 60 plywood pieces. This will be

the opening from the henhouse to the run. The edges of the openings should be 22 inches from the open side of the henhouse and 28 inches from the bottom of the storage base. Enlist the help of a friend for the last steps.

6. Screw the 48 x 60-inch plywood piece with the opening into the storage base, storage cupboard, and henhouse frames.

7. Screw the other 48 x 60-inch plywood piece with no opening into the back side of the storage base, storage cupboard, and henhouse.

8. Using a large drill bit, drill holes roughly 1 to $1^1/_2$ inches in size along the top of the henhouse walls. This allows for good ventilation.

9. Screw two hinges (for the storage cupboard) onto one 36 x 25-inch piece of plywood and attach to the cupboard storage area. This is the door to this area.

10. Screw two hinges (for the henhouse) onto the other 36 x 25-inch piece of plywood and attach to the henhouse area. This is the henhouse door.

11. Adjust latches to both the cupboard and the henhouse doors.

12. Carefully cut and position the corrugated metal roofing over the henhouse and cupboard storage area. You can also ask your hardware store if they can cut it to size for you. Hammer into place.

13. Carefully cut and position the corrugated metal roofing over the chicken run. You can also ask your hardware store if they can cut it to size for you. Hammer into place.

14. Move chicken run into place against the henhouse and storage structure. Use latches to hold the run and henhouse together so you can disassemble it into two pieces when it needs to be moved.

Three bantam hens can comfortably live in this worm bin/chicken coop combo design. Add the used chicken bedding right into the worm bin with your kitchen scraps.

Each of the three pieces—worm bin, henhouse, and run—can be removed and easily transported to your next homestead. Use untreated, naturally rot-resistant lumber like cedar or redwood.

Constructing the Chicken Run

Materials
- Four 2 x 4s, 4 feet long
- Ten 2 x 4s, 2 feet long
- Two 2 x 2s, 2 feet long
- Two 2 x 2s, 13 $^3/_4$ inches long
- Wire mesh, 2 feet wide
- Two metal hinges
- Poultry staples
- One-pound box of wood screws

1. Begin to construct the top frame of the run by screwing two 2 x 4s that are 4 feet long to two 2 x 4s that are 2 feet long.
2. Repeat step one to create the bottom of the frame for the run.

3. Position four of the 2 x 4s that are 2 feet long to each corner of the top and bottom frame pieces. This should create a box.
4. Add extra support along the 4-feet-long sides of the frame by screwing in two additional 2 x 4s that have been cut to 2 feet long.
5. Hammer in wire mesh with the poultry staples along all sides except one of the 2 x 2 ends. This is where the door to the run will be.
6. Construct the door to the run by screwing the four 2 x 2 pieces together to make a square. Hammer wire mesh to the door with poultry staples.
7. With the help of a friend, screw in hinges to the door of the run and attach to the end of the run.

Constructing the Henhouse

Materials
- Four 2 x 2s, 24 inches long
- Four 2 x 2s, 20 inches long
- Four 2 x 2s, 21 inches long
- One $1/2$-inch-thick plywood piece, cut 24 x 23 inches (base)
- Two $1/2$-inch-thick plywood pieces, cut $24^1/2$ x 25 inches (sides)
- One $1/2$-inch-thick plywood piece, cut 23 x 25 inches (front)
- One $1/2$-inch-thick plywood piece, cut $24^1/2$ x 25 inches (back door)
- Two metal hinges
- Corrugated metal roofing, standard $26^1/2$ inch wide, cut 27 inches long
- One-pound box of wood screws

1. Create the frame of the henhouse by screwing together the 2 x 2s to make a box, with one side slightly taller than the opposite.
2. Cut a 12 x 12-inch opening into the base piece of plywood, which allows the chickens to enter the henhouse from down below in the chicken run.
3. Screw the base plywood piece onto the bottom of the henhouse frame.
4. Screw the side plywood pieces onto the side frames of the henhouse.
5. With the help of a friend, screw the hinges into place on the back door of the henhouse and attach to the shorter side of the frame.
6. Screw the front piece of plywood onto the taller side of the frame.
7. Position the corrugated metal over the top of the henhouse and hammer into the sidewalls to secure. It should hang off the front and back slightly, to prevent water from dripping in.

Constructing the Worm Bin

Materials

- Four 2 x 2s, 9 inches long
- Four 2 x 2s, 23 inches long
- Four 2 x 2s, $21\frac{1}{2}$ inches long
- Two $\frac{1}{2}$-inch-thick plywood pieces, cut 12 x $24\frac{1}{2}$ inches (sides)
- Two $\frac{1}{2}$-inch-thick plywood pieces, cut 12 x 24 inches (ends)
- Two $\frac{1}{2}$-inch-thick plywood pieces, cut $25\frac{1}{2}$ x 24 inches (top and bottom)
- Two metal hinges with screws no longer than $\frac{1}{2}$ inch
- Two handles
- One-pound box of wood screws

1. Screw the 2 x 2s together to make a box that is 24 x 24 x 9 inches deep.
2. Screw the plywood side pieces onto the side of the frame.
3. Screw the plywood end pieces onto the ends of the frame.
4. Screw the bottom plywood piece onto the bottom of the frame.
5. With the help of a friend, screw the hinges onto the top of the worm bin and into the top of the frame.
6. Screw the two handles onto opposite sides of the worm bin.
7. Using a drill with a 1 to $1\frac{1}{2}$-inch bit, drill large holes along the top of the sides of the worm bin for aeration.

The worm bin and henhouse latch onto the run. All three pieces can be unlatched for easy moving.

Assembling the Minicoop

Materials

- Three metal latches

1. Place the chicken run in a flat area. Place the worm bin and henhouse on either side of the top of the coop.
2. Attach metal latches to connect the worm bin to the run and the henhouse to the run. These can be unlatched when the pieces need to be moved separately.

I live in the city and am therefore limited as to how many chickens I can keep. Because of this, I personally enjoy a mix of breeds in my small flock—different feather coloring and different egg colors. It is completely acceptable for us to take the aesthetics of our flocks into consideration when making these decisions.

Commercial egg farms often have crossbreeds that have been engineered to be prolific layers. The downside to these birds is that they are generally not very personable and sometimes skittish. In terms of chicken brains, they also tend to be rather dim. Their life span may be shorter because they burn themselves out with that constant pressure to lay, lay, lay.

Backyard breeds are good overall layers, reaching their peak egg production during their first year of laying and often providing an egg a day while taking a day off about once a week. Depending on the breed, it is typical for production to decline slightly in the second and third years. Their egg production will continue to decline over the years, but you can still expect the occasional egg from an older bird well into her fifth or even eighth year before she quits laying altogether.

In the city, we keep chickens as a hobby for a food source, nitrogen-rich manure, and entertainment, so a backyard hen does not necessarily lose her value when she decides to retire from the egg business. As an alternative to butchering older hens, consider adding a couple new hens to your flock every two to three years to keep a diversity of ages. This type of flock management eases the burden of an old hen, ensuring you will always have a steady egg supply from the younger gals.

Some may choose to butcher an old hen, but be cautioned that the term "tough old bird" became an everyday saying for a reason. She will not be good for much more than stew meat, but at the very least you will be eating an animal that enjoyed a happy life in the sun, eating good food and scratching around in the dirt.

Obtaining Chickens
Adult hens can be purchased through online classifieds, online poultry forums, or from the local feed store. Some feed stores only sell chicks, while others sell both babies and adult birds. Ask whether they plan to carry chickens during the spring or whether they sell poultry year-round.

Generally, chicks are available in the spring and summer from feed stores, year-round from mail-order catalogs, and sometimes at local farms in the warmer months. Catalog sales often require a minimum of twenty-five chicks per order, so perhaps you can find some friends to go in together on an order. If you are looking for only a handful of peeps, the feed store and local farms are your best bets. Call around the various feed stores in your area to find out who will have the largest selection of chicken breeds.

Raising Chicks
Raising chicks is a rewarding and entertaining experience that requires a bit

more work than caring for grown hens. Typically, buying chicks means you have a wider selection of breeds to choose from. Once grown, these chickens will often be friendlier and more accustomed to handling. I have heard stories of such friendly chickens happily climbing in the laps of their owners and even sneaking in through the back door to leisurely hang out on the couch. Be warned that they are not housebroken!

When picking out baby chicks, look for bright-eyed, perky birds that are actively running around eating and drinking. Slower chicks, especially droopy-headed chicks, may be weaker and therefore less likely to thrive. Their lethargy can be a sign of internal problems or disease. Spare yourself the painful experience by hedging your bets with the strongest birds.

Baby chicks are sold as either straight run or sexed. Sexed chicks mean you have roughly a 75 percent chance that your baby is a girl. They sex them all, but there is still room for error. That is why it is recommended you buy four chicks if you want to end up with three hens—someone will most likely turn out to be a rooster. You can also opt for unsexed, straight run chicks, which are cheaper, and choose to make a meal out of the roosters, keeping the hens for eggs. In that case, plan on 50 percent being males and 50 percent being females.

When ordering from a catalog, your post office will call you as soon as your livestock order arrives. They will be quite eager for you to pick the babies up as soon as possible, due to the "chirp, chirp, chirp" noises coming from the box. Make sure everything is ready prior to the birds' arrival. If your new chicks seem droopy, feed them a mixture of one quart water to $1/3$ cup sugar to perk them up and soothe their distress.

Chicks need a few special supplies set up and ready before they come home with you, either from a feed store or catalog order. A brooder is a small temporary house for the chicks where they will live for the first six to twelve weeks, until their fuzzy chick feathers have been replaced by adult feathers. The brooder should be well-ventilated, but protect the chicks from drafts. The enclosure needs to offer protection from predators (including house pets), provide adequate space, and include a heat source.

A wooden box or cardboard container can work well as a makeshift brooder. The floor of the brooder should not be smooth or slick, as chicks have a hard time standing well. I would also avoid wire mesh flooring, which can expose chicks to drafts and also increase the likelihood of coccidiosis, a common disease affecting young chickens. The size of the brooder needs to increase as the birds increase in size to make sure everyone has enough wing room.

The ideal temperature for newly hatched chicks is approximately 95 degrees Fahrenheit, which you can achieve with a heat lamp and 250-watt bulb. You can also use a light fixture with a reflector dome around it and an incandescent bulb if you are raising fewer

than fifty chicks. With either method, securely place the lamp at least eighteen inches away from the litter. Make sure the lamp does not touch anything flammable, as it will get hot to the touch and is a fire hazard.

Pay very close attention to the chicks to read their cue on the temperature level and raise/lower the heat source accordingly. They are too cold if they huddle under the light. They are getting too hot when the chicks are scattered around the fringe of the brooder. The chicks are comfortable when they are active, eating, and drinking, and are evenly dispersed in the brooder.

Just as chickens can suffer from the cold, too much heat is also too much of a good thing. Make sure your chicks have a space of about two to three feet around the heat source so they can move away if they get too warm.

After the first week, begin lowering the temperature in the brooder by five degrees each week until it reaches room temperature. As they begin to feather out and the temperature in the brooder is lowered, you can take them outside on mild days for some supervised play. A neighbor cat or circling hawk can do quick damage to a young chicken, so keep a very close eye on the flock.

Light should be provided to the chicks for twenty-four hours during their first couple days, but then adjust the light to mimic the sun. This can be done naturally by placing them near a draft-free window or artificially with an indoor light set on a timer.

Chicks should be fed commercial chick starter to ensure optimum health and development. Chick starter has higher protein content than adult chicken feed. Never feed them egg-layer feed, as the calcium in this feed can seriously damage their delicate kidneys. Follow the feeding

recommendations on the chick starter, which should include some guidance on when to transition to adult feed. The food should be kept in a shallow, open dish for the first couple days as the chicks explore what to eat. After about a week, begin to use a regular feeder to help keep them from walking into the food and scratching it out and all over the brooder.

During your chicks' first few days, use paper towels in the brooder as the bedding. This gives them some traction for walking around, which prevents incorrect leg formation. It also prevents them from eating the bedding as they learn where the food and beverage is in this chick pad. Transition to bedding material like shredded newspaper or pine shavings after these first two or three days. Change the bedding often to keep their home clean and dry.

When they first arrive in their new home, dip their beaks into the water container to help them learn what it is and where it is located in the brooder. Keep it close to the new chicks in an enclosed container, which will prevent them from walking through it. Miniwaterers especially made for chicks are available at feed stores. An open water container both increases their chance of getting a chill and contaminating the water.

Baby chicks can be left unattended for hours at a time when you are working or sleeping at night. Just check in on them periodically throughout the day.

At four to six weeks, introduce a roost into the brooder. Position the bar low enough for the birds to easily jump on and off so they can experiment with keeping their balance. It is pretty hilarious to watch them play with their new toy, but over time they should learn on their own to sleep on the roost at night. Help them along by gently setting them up there when the lights go out. It may take several attempts over a few nights, but they will eventually figure it out.

Troubled Chick

Sadly, 5 percent of baby chicks die during their first seven weeks of life—a misfortune many chickenkeepers experience. Pasting, or sticky bottoms, is a common, yet preventable, cause. This typically occurs when chicks are chilly, overheated, or improperly fed. Soft droppings stick to their vent, which is the area of feathers over the anus. The vent area hardens and becomes blocked, leading to death. Gently pick off the hardened area and increase their protein intake by combining chick starter with an equal amount of cornmeal or crushed, uncooked oatmeal. Some chickenkeepers feed their baby chicks this combination for the first three days to prevent pasting from even occurring.

Perhaps the most common cause of chick fatalities is a condition called coccidiosis, or cocci, for short. Protozoa are natural bacteria that colonize in chicken intestines. They become problematic when the levels of the bacteria get out of control and overcolonize, usually because a chick nibbled too many droppings in food, water, or bedding. Typically this affects chicks around three to six weeks of age. You decrease the likelihood of this affecting your flock if you keep conditions clean.

Sometimes a baby chick dies and there is no way to prevent it. For example, if pasting occurs later than one week of age, there may be an intestinal problem. In other cases, there may be an internal growth problem or genetic issue that leads to death.

You can help your chicks thrive by providing adequate, clean living conditions and constant access to clean food and water. Consider feeding the chicks a probiotic formula for the first few weeks. These beneficial bacteria and yeasts colonize in their intestines and fend off harmful organisms. You can purchase formula from feed stores and sprinkle it onto their food or simply provide a little live-culture yogurt for them to eat.

I brought home a batch of baby chicks one spring and knew right away I had a runt. As hard as I tried to nurse her along, she stayed much smaller than the other healthy girls, who were over twice her size after a few weeks. I never gave up hope, eventually resorting to feeding her mashed feed and water with an eye dropper. I surprised myself at how hard I cried when she finally passed away, and I found myself wishing there was something else I could have done for her.

It is a sad thing to lose a chick to death, and sometimes there is nothing you could have done differently to prevent it from happening. Do the best you can and know that nature is a more powerful force in some cases.

Puberty

In the first couple months of growth, you will notice gender signs in your chickens. Cockerels, which are young males, develop reddened combs and wattles around this time. Combs are the rubbery-looking areas on their forehead, and wattles hang underneath their beaks. You may hear some rather pathetic attempts at crowing from them, but they soon get the hang of things and belt out some strong *cockle-doodle-doos*, or *coo-cooroo-kookoo*, for Spanish-speaking chickens, after a couple weeks of practice. Hens will begin laying eggs somewhere between four and six months of age.

When the chicks are fully feathered out and no baby fuzz remains, it's time to get them used to the great outdoors. You have spent the last several weeks lowering the temperature in their brooder to match the outside temperatures, so they should be adjusted to the weather. Begin taking them out to their coop for a few hours each day, gradually increasing the amount of time they spend outside.

My husband, Jay, and I felt like proud parents when our gangly teenage hens got to finally experience the great outdoors. We stayed close to them as they ran around tasting their first worms and blades of grass. After a few days, they learned the ropes of their new digs and were ready to move in. They grow up so fast!

Health and Safety

If you are raising chickens in the city, it is likely that your biggest issue will be predators rather than disease. Urban predators come in the form of loose neighborhood dogs, clever raccoons, and sneaky opossums. Rats and mice may become a nuisance issue if food is left on the floor of the coop, but they generally do little damage to a grown chicken. Cats are rarely a bother as they are similar in size to an adult chicken. Chickens can hold their own with their prehistoric talons and sharp beaks. The other critters are the primary culprits in chicken fatalities.

Old bedding is removed once a week and replaced with new, dry bedding.

Take caution when designing the coop by considering ways to foil predators. Discourage animals from digging under the coop by extending the fencing twelve inches underground. It is common to have a small door on the henhouse so the flock is safely locked up every night and let out in the morning. Consider stronger deterrents like electric fencing around the outside of the coop or using motor-sensor sprinklers if you have particularly determined predators. Once an animal kills a chicken, expect it to relentlessly come back for second helpings.

A reduction in egg laying can be the most noticeable sign of disease affecting your flock. Diseases will always be present, but they typically only affect your flock when the birds are stressed. Hunching, hanging head, dull or ruffled feathers, weight loss, and decreased egg production are all symptoms of possible disease.

Enteric diseases affect the digestive system; its symptoms are loose or bloody droppings, weakness, loss of appetite, increased thirst, and dehydration. Signs of respiratory diseases include labored breathing, coughing, sneezing, sniffling, gasping, and runny eyes.

Parasites are nasty little buggers that may come into contact with your chickens, whether rural or urban. Internal bugs, like worms and such, are usually only a problem when chickens have unsanitary living conditions. But you are going to be a good, responsible chickenkeeper, so we won't focus on these guys. Instead, external parasites like fleas and mites are the ones to watch for.

If you keep your coop dry and clean, with a routine change of bedding, you can help prevent these creepy crawlies from ever taking root. A dry dirt floor that allows your flock to take dust baths will also cut down on your chances of having these bugs move in. Inspect your flock regularly, perhaps once every other week or once a month, to check for bugs.

Lice will be visible on the skin and feathers of your birds, often causing chickens to pull out feathers from irritation. Mites will live on the skin or feathers of your birds as well, leaving traces like blood spots, scabs, or darkened grime on feathers, especially around the vent. Feed stores sell various dusting powders you can spread around the coop to rid the area of both lice and mites. Scaly leg mites live under the scales of chicken legs, so you will see the scales actually pushed up a bit from the surface. Applying petroleum jelly to the legs will suffocate the bugs.

I do an annual deep cleaning of my coop to reduce the risk of disease and parasites. When the weather is nice at the beginning of the summer, I let the girls free range in the backyard all day. Meanwhile, I rake out all of the bedding from both the run and henhouse. I then spray white vinegar on all the walls and ceilings. I do a thorough scrubbing of all surfaces with white vinegar as well. Everything is then allowed to air dry for the rest of the day. Once dry, I add in fresh bedding and restock all of their supplies.

It is not mandatory to do an annual cleaning like this, but I actually enjoy it.

It makes me feel like the chickens get a spring cleaning as I do my own spring cleaning inside. It's simply an added precaution that helps me maintain a healthy and happy flock.

As the cold season approaches, your flock will begin to prepare for the change in temperature through a process called molting. Old feathers are replaced with new ones, generally in about three weeks. The birds are never fully naked, but will instead be a little shaggy and patchy looking during this time. The new feathers ensure they have a thick coat to keep cold breezes from penetrating to their skin. They will also fluff those feathers up at night, creating pockets underneath to hold their body heat in.

A little extra weight on your chickens is not a bad idea in the cold season, assuming it is done in moderation. We don't want overweight chickens, just slightly plump ones. Adding some extra helpings of scratch to their winter diet ensures they have enough protein to keep their energy levels up, as they expend more energy trying to keep their body temperatures high. Keep a thick layer of bedding in the coop during these cold months as well. This provides a snug spot for them to nuzzle into to escape the chills.

During hot spells, keep cold and clean water present at all times. Make sure the flock always has access to shady areas as well. Putting out a few different water containers will make it easier for your birds to stay cool without working too hard to get access to water.

Breeds well-suited for cold weather

typically are heavier, larger standard breeds. These include Brahma, Cochin, New Hampshire, Orphington, Plymouth Rock, Rhode Island Red, and Wyandotte. Chickenkeepers living in hot climates should consider lighter breeds like Andalusian, Buttercup, Hamburg, Leghorn, Minorca, Naked Neck, Shamo, and Spanish.

Every chickenkeeper has a different opinion of how cold is too cold for a chicken. I live in the mild Pacific Northwest, and my chickens are not accustomed to really cold winters (nor am I, for that matter). If the temperature drops below 20 degrees Fahrenheit, I get concerned, add more bedding, and give them warm water a couple times a day. If it gets into the teens, I move them into my enclosed back porch and enjoy the petting zoo until it warms up a bit.

Those who live in northern areas tell me anything above zero is still okay for the chickens. These folks build insulated coops from the get-go to prepare for the cold weather and place cardboard against the wire walls of the run to hold in heat. They carefully watch for frostbite on their chickens' combs, but the chickens do fine.

As you begin your chickenkeeping venture, find a local vet who has livestock experience. Chickens are becoming more popular again in urban areas, so maybe you can find a vet close by who has experience with them. Having a vet's information in advance is good for emergencies. You may never need it; sometimes the advice of a fellow chickenkeeper or feed store owner is enough to help you navigate problems.

Chickensitting

Your flock of chickens will probably be okay on their own if you need to leave town for the weekend, but it is always a good security measure to have a friend drop by once a day for egg collection. This is an opportunity to make sure no critters have dug into the coop and the girls haven't accidentally tipped their water over.

You will need to enlist the help of a chickensitter when you plan to leave town for a week or more. This can be a friendly neighbor or one of your buddies. They will still need to drop by once a day to check on food and water levels and collect eggs. They will also need to change the coop bedding once a week in your absence.

In my experience, it makes whoever is chickensitting feel more comfortable if they can come over about a week in advance and watch you do the weekly maintenance. I think this is because they really don't realize keeping chickens is actually that simple. It takes me about ten to fifteen minutes to do the weekly maintenance: changing bedding, refilling grit and oyster shell, rinsing out and refilling the water and food containers. It gives sitters peace of mind, though, and gets them used to the funny cluckers.

I have never had much trouble finding a chickensitter because my friends are easily won over with homegrown organic eggs. Save up a dozen in advance, or let them reap the rewards on their own each evening when they drop by for egg duty. Throwing in a jar of delicious preserves always goes a long way as well. Having a homestead is also about community, and this can be a great way to introduce your friends and neighbors to the joys of modern homesteading.

Online City Critter Community

It is one thing to put a plant in the ground and risk failing. It's another thing to move a flock of chickens into the backyard and risk not doing it right. These are living, squawking (or quacking or baaing) creatures that depend almost exclusively on you for survival. I know you can do it, but I also know it feels safer to do it with the help of experts nearby.

The feed store can be a great resource for getting advice on keeping backyard livestock, but they may not have the best advice when it comes to ultra-urban issues like a cranky next-door neighbor or local city codes. Establishing a virtual community of urban farmers can be a great substitute for the real thing. Go online and seek them out while you wait to stumble upon another neighbor keeping backyard livestock.

Listservs are becoming increasingly popular and are often specific to different communities. Often you need to write the group moderator to gain access to the group, which is usually a safety precaution intended to keep spammers out. You can set up your account preferences to get an e-mail every time someone posts a new topic, or never receive e-mails and instead just check the website periodically for new discussions.

These are great places to find out about local breeders, who often post on these Listservs when they have livestock available for purchase. It's a better bet for them that their animals end up in good, knowledgeable homes rather than risking their livestock with the masses by advertising them in online classifieds.

Often discussions include things of interest to urban livestock keepers such as feed sources, problem-solving illness, or unusual animal behaviors. You may be surprised to discover that after crying over the keyboard as you lament the loss of a beloved hen to a sneaky raccoon, you receive an outpouring of support and similar stories from other members. Likewise, they will be there to celebrate that jubilant moment of your first homegrown egg. They can be an incredibly valuable resource for guidance and support.

Take a bold dive into the blogosphere to connect with other modern homesteaders who have critters in the backyard. There are tons of us out there documenting our trials and triumphs in an effort to share information and resources and to learn from each other's experiences. Often blogs will include a list of the author's favorite blogs, so you can keep digging deeper and deeper into this Web community. Ask questions in the comments section and start attending local events that get posted.

Duck Tales

Ducks are slowly building a reputation as an efficient and low-maintenance back-yard poultry option. They lay eggs that are approximately 25 percent larger than chickens', with the best breeds laying more eggs per year than their chicken cousins. They provide excellent pest control when it comes to managing slugs, snails, mosquitoes, grasshoppers, and other bugs. They are also avid foragers and can considerably reduce your over-all feed costs. Ducks also generally suffer fewer diseases than chickens, making them a hardier poultry option.

Part of their low-maintenance reputation comes from ducks' ability to with-stand wet conditions and colder climates due to their thick coats of oily feathers. With the help of these down coats, they can comfortably tolerate temperatures well below freezing.

More than chickens, ducks benefit from being able to free range in the back-yard. If you have a little more space than a postage-stamp yard or happen to live in a really cold climate with harsh win-ters, ducks will be a wonderful addition to your backyard homestead. Apartment dwellers with a balcony should stick to a small flock of bantam chickens.

Ducks love to be outside eating grasses, insects, and playing in the water. Domes-tic breeds are not terrific flyers and can be easily contained to a yard with a three-foot fence. They generously provide natu-ral pest control and nitrogen-rich garden fertilizer. Keep them away from delicate vegetables like greens, which they will gobble up. They are also berry aficionados,

so protect ground-covering strawberries or berry bushes within bill's reach.

Ducks 101

Every duck's personality varies, but in general they are calm, docile creatures. This is especially true when they are

Chicken egg (left) compared to a duck egg (right).

raised from ducklings and socialized to humans at an early age. If you think baby chicks are cute, wait until you handle a duckling—they are absolutely adorable.

Their oil-producing gland is located near the base of their tail. Ducks squeeze this gland with their bill and distribute oil through their feathers throughout the day. Performing this maintenance regime prevents water from penetrating their coats and gives them a glossy, clean appearance.

Male ducks are called drakes and females are referred to as hens. As is the case with all poultry, males are needed only if you want to make bird babies. Females will lay unfertilized eggs without a male present. Whereas roosters make too much noise for city living, drakes make no additional noise and could be feasible in a backyard flock. Generally one male to five or six females is a good ratio for breeding.

Like chickens, ducks have a pecking order to maintain. If you choose to add to the existing flock, be prepared for some squabbling as everyone sorts out his or her place.

Keeping ducks in the backyard is gaining in popularity, and most cities that allow chickens will also include other poultry, like ducks, under the same provision. It is always a good idea to check with your local extension office or zoning department to understand the current laws for your city before you acquire your flock.

Making Peace

Talking to the neighbors about your duck endeavor is highly recommended, whether you need their formal permission or not. Ducks are a little noisier than chickens, so your neighbors may hear occasional quacking. You may find your

Duck housing can be very simple and rustic.

flock quacks a bit more when you come outside as they begin to associate your presence with delicious treats. If you have close neighbors, look for quieter breeds like Khaki Campbells, Welsh Harlequins, or Anconas.

Be sure to discuss your plans for minimizing any barnyard smells with frequent duck house maintenance. Keeping an open door on communication will ensure neighbors come to you to complain first rather than filing a nuisance report with the city. And it can't be said enough, a little egg bribing always goes a long way with reluctant neighbors.

Housing

Ducks often prefer to be outside during the day and through the night, so their needs can be simpler than that of chickens. You should give them the option of using a sheltered area for escaping the elements: strong winds, cold nights, or hot afternoons. In urban settings, the duck house is also a place to escape predators like raccoons, opossums, and loose dogs, so closing them up at night in the duck house is strongly recommended.

Inside the duck house should be a nesting box for laying eggs. This makes the eggs easy to find and collect, and also keeps them clean. Similar to that for chickens, the nesting box should be about twelve inches square. One nesting box per four hens should be adequate.

The overall size of the duck house should range between two and six square feet per duck. No roosting bars are needed, as ducks prefer to sleep on the ground. Wire flooring can be hard on their feet, especially with larger breeds, so use a solid floor if possible. Plan to use straw or pine shavings as bedding to collect droppings and keep the flock cozy. My friends made a duck house that is movable, so they do not use bedding other than the lawn. They just move it every few days to a new spot in the yard.

Free-ranging ducks are not as destructive in the garden as chickens when it comes to hardier vegetables that are fairly well established. Ducks prefer to seek out protein (insects) before dining at the salad bar. Their webbed feet make it difficult for them to rake up the soil as well as chickens do with their clawed feet. In muddy conditions, ducks may root around in the soil, but they will not scratch up dry dirt.

A pool of water for swimming is not necessary for your flock, but they will certainly enjoy themselves if one is provided.

They can stay cleaner and entertain themselves for hours by swimming around. Jay and I call it the never-ending pool party, and it sure does look like fun.

Many people reuse old bathtubs, cattle feeders, or kiddie pools. Laying down a bed of sand about four inches thick for the pool to rest on will keep the area well drained, but is not mandatory. The water needs to have an easy point of exit for the birds, as they can drown if they get stuck in the pool.

Use your imagination when it comes to the ducky water park. I have seen pools lined with bricks or slabs of flagstone along the banks to give them a more natural appearance. Maybe you could construct a Moroccan-inspired tiled bathtub submerged in a shady corner of the garden. Whatever your fancy, keep in mind your little birds will also deposit little poops in the pool. Be ready to change the water regularly so the birds are kept clean. Ducks should not be swimming and drinking in mucky water. And, if a pool won't work for your space, provide a bucket so they can at least wash their faces and get a little water fix.

If your yard is simply ill-suited for free-ranging ducks, you can keep them enclosed in a space of ten to twenty-five square feet per bird. Breeds that work well in confinement are Call, East Indie, Australian Spotted, Muscovy, and Pekin ducks. A better solution, though, may be exploring another backyard poultry option like chickens, which require less space.

Khaki Campbells make great backyard ducks.

Ducks, like other farm animals, need company.

Supplies

Like other poultry, ducks break down food using their gizzard. You will need to provide a source of grit, or small rocks, they can eat when needed and store in their gizzard. If the ducks are allowed to free range in a substantial area, they will most likely pick up the grit they need from the ground. However, providing a constant, additional source is a good idea.

Ducks need access to commercial feed at all times. Hanging feeders work best to store feed and dispense as it is eaten. Keeping the feeder off the ground helps it stay dry and clean. The same goes for a water container, which needs to be provided at all times.

Feed your flock of ducks leafy greens in addition to commercial feed. This can come in the form of kitchen scraps or perhaps you could plant an extra row of kale in your garden each year just for the ducks. Leafy greens like dandelion leaves, lettuce, and tender grasses will provide more vitamins and nutrients for your flock, adding to their overall health and happiness. It will also make their eggs taste even richer!

Choosing Breeds

There are more than twenty breeds of domestic ducks raised in North America, and several are well-suited for the backyard. If you are not providing a pool of water for your flock, consider colored breeds that will have an overall cleaner appearance.

Lightweight breeds are generally the best egg layers and are nonbroody. They are better suited for life on land and are active foragers. They also tend to be poor flyers, which means you can avoid annual wing trimming.

The most popular breed from this class that is perhaps best suited for the backyard is Campbells. This breed was developed in England in the 1800s, and they have developed a reputation as prolific layers. The variety most commonly found now are Khaki Campbells, which have a lovely beige coloring.

Another lightweight breed is the Welsh Harlequin, which is somewhat rare. The males have green heads with white bodies, and the females are all white. They are lovely birds and good layers with reportedly calm demeanors. You may be more likely to find them in mail-order catalogs instead of the local feed store.

Runners are a popular lightweight backyard breed that have a unique appearance and high egg-laying productivity.

They stand upright and do not have a waddle in their walk. Their nickname is "bottle neck" because their body has an overall upright bottle appearance. This breed originated in Scotland in the early 1900s and comes in a variety of colors: chocolate, black, fawn, blue, and white. They are very active foragers, quick on their feet, and add an interesting, attractive look to the backyard flock. They are Jay's favorite backyard poultry option because they are so funny looking.

Medium-weight breeds are typically dual purpose, meaning you can raise them for meat and eggs. Orpingtons are a good overall variety with a moderate temperament. Heavyweight breeds are primarily for meat only. Beginning backyard urban homesteaders interested in eggs should stick to the lightweight breeds.

Obtaining Ducks

Local feed stores, catalog hatcheries, and online poultry communities are your best sources for obtaining either ducklings or adult birds. Be warned that nothing is cuter than a baby duck. Raising them from babies means they will be better socialized.

When shopping for ducklings, look for active, perky birds. If you order from a hatchery, you may need to go in with a few friends on an order. They will most likely have a minimum order larger than an urban keeper needs. As mentioned before, they may also have the best selection of breeds to choose from.

Runners are a quirky upright breed often called bottle necks.

Raising Ducklings

Ducks are said to be the easiest fowl to raise, as they have generally low mortality rates. Increase your chances for success by having all your supplies ready prior to the feathered friends moving in. It is far more enjoyable to just watch the entertaining ducklings for hours and hours instead of running all over town getting supplies together.

The first thing ducklings will need is a brooder—a temporary home that is free from drafts and stays warm. The brooder will need to increase in size as the ducks grow. Allow for roughly a square foot per bird for the first two weeks. Increase that to about two square feet per bird from the second to fourth week. After the fourth week, give them somewhere between three and five square feet per bird.

Locate the brooder in a safe area of your house (i.e., away from the cat or dog). They need a safe, predator-proof place to call home. Hopefully you can find a great place that does not require enclosing the entire brooder. Fresh air is healthier for your birds.

After about the third or fourth week, the ducks can start exploring life outside the brooder. Keep a very close eye on them—they are still small and fairly defenseless against cats and other bullies. Take them out only during mild weather until they get older and beefier.

The brooder should have a porcelain heat lamp that holds a 250-watt bulb. Hang this about eighteen to twenty-four inches above the brooder and watch the birds closely. They are too warm and the

light needs to be raised if they all scatter to the fringe of the brooder. Lower the lamp a bit to keep them warmer if they huddle in the middle or pile on top of each other. The ducklings are comfortable if they are moving around freely, balancing active times with nap time, eating, and drinking.

Ducklings need less heat than baby chickens, probably around 90 degrees Fahrenheit to start. Lower the temperature about five degrees each week. When they are six to eight weeks old, the ducks

are considered adolescents and can handle temperatures of around 50 degrees Fahrenheit. They continue to get hardier as they grow into adults.

The bedding in the brooder can consist of a number of materials: wood shavings, chopped straw, peanut shells, and other nut shells. They will need a thick layer of bedding, around three to six inches deep, as they will be messy with the water and spill it around. Thick bedding means you can stir it around to keep things dry. Be ready to change it out frequently as it becomes soiled.

As cute as it is to see baby ducklings paddling away in your bathtub, hold off on any swimming activity until they are about two weeks old. By that time, they will be a little stronger and well adjusted to life outside the eggshell. Two-week-old fuzzy ducklings are still incredibly adorable.

Have a ready supply of duckling-sized grit, starter duck feed, and clean drinking water. Add in some fresh greens to mix up their diet and give them additional vitamins and nutrients they may be missing from the commercial feed.

Health and Safety

As with any backyard livestock, think carefully about the potential predators that travel through urban areas. Rats and mice will be pests that eat your duck feed, but most likely they will not harm the birds. Raccoons, opossums, and stray dogs and cats can become potential problems, though.

If you let the ducks free range during the day, do it in a fenced yard to decrease the likelihood of a dog wandering through to discover dinner. Also consider a latched door on the duck house so it gets closed up at night and opened in the morning.

Compared to chickens, ducks have a much healthier resistance to disease and parasites—part of the reason they are gaining such popularity in the backyard homestead. Typically, infectious diseases are caused by overcrowding, unsanitary living conditions, or an inadequate diet.

Prevent illness in your flock by providing a balanced diet, clean digs, and constant access to clean water.

Be mindful of toxin sources in your backyard. Do not leave out things the birds can ingest that would be harmful, like chemicals, moldy food scraps, etc. Just be smart and attentive to their basic needs.

Just like for any backyard livestock, search around in advance for a local vet who has experience with livestock. This may be someone local or you might have to drive a little ways to the rural outskirts of town to visit the vet. Most likely you can rely on the feed store owner or online communities of poultrykeepers to steer you in the right direction when problems arise. It's always better to be prepared, though.

Ducksitting

Ducks, like other poultry, can be okay on their own for a few days here and there without you around. Your biggest concern is making sure they are safe from predators. Have a friend or neighbor check in with the flock once a day to collect eggs and restock food and water when needed.

Housing should still be cleaned out about once a week, so train a buddy before you leave on vacation to do this while you are gone. Have them come over one afternoon to watch you do it. They may just start keeping their own flock when they realize how simple the whole process is. Be sure to bake up some goodies from your fresh duck eggs to thank them for their help.

Totes My Goats

Raising milk goats is a topic that is becoming increasingly interesting to homesteaders, but goats are not a great choice for everyone. Goats need a sizable backyard, so apartment and condo dwellers may need to put this idea on hold for a couple years. It is also important that future goatkeepers understand that goats are truly farm animals, not pets, and should be raised as such. Goats are smart, very curious creatures that like structure and routine.

Keeping goats for milk is a serious commitment and a decision that should be made with careful thought. You are committing to milking them twice a day for roughly ten months of the year—rain, shine, sleet, or snow. When you go on vacation, the goats do not. They still need to be milked at regular intervals. Foster a strong network of goatsitting friends who can lend a hand when you go on vacation. Neighbors who own a small herd of goats can work well.

The word *goats*, plural, is being used because they are herd animals and therefore very social creatures. They should never be raised alone, so plan to have at least two together. They will get incredibly lonely and let you know they are unhappy by acting out and being all-around difficult. Again, goats are actually very smart, clever creatures.

Two standard goats will need a decent-sized, securely fenced, space, while a couple miniature goats require slightly less real estate. A goat yard roughly 20 x 20 feet in size will be ample space for a pair of does. You can get by with around 20 x 15 feet for two miniatures. In exchange for clean and safe living conditions, they will reward you with fresh, homegrown milk that can be used for drinking, ice cream, butter, yogurt, or cheese.

Goats can also give something back to the garden in the form of manure. When you clean out the goat house and yard, all of that used bedding and manure will grow some very robust vegetables.

Goats are curious, entertaining, and very intelligent creatures.

Goats 101

Boy goats are called bucks, and girl goats are called does. Babies and young goats are referred to as kids. Goats have gotten a bad reputation for being stinky animals, but this is not quite true. Bucks have scent glands near their horns, and their smell is strongest during mating season in the fall. Does, on the other hand, have no such scent glands.

You will most likely keep two does and no bucks if you plan to keep goats for milk. Assuming you maintain a good cleaning regime, barnyard smells should not be an issue.

Goats are similar to deer in that both prefer to browse rather than graze. Although they will do some grazing off the ground, they prefer things a few feet higher, like shrubs and trees. A common misconception is that goats make great lawn mowers. Although they munch a little grass here and there, they require a varied diet and will be more interested in plant material above the ground. They love variety and are naturally curious creatures. They have gotten a bad rap as being willing to eat everything in sight, when really they are just willing to *try* everything at least once. Leaves, flowers, and bark, especially on young trees, are all up for taste testing.

Due to their curious nature and preference for variety, they would love nothing more than the opportunity to explore your lovely garden and snack on all those delicious vegetables. Only the sturdiest fences will keep them contained in the goat yard, so don't skimp on cheap

A lazy afternoon spent munching and napping.

materials when you build their living quarters. I have seen many goats stand up against the fence, or even bat at the fence, to both test its strength and get a better view outside the goat yard.

Some goat breeds are naturally hornless, but most need to be debudded, or dehorned, when they are young. A horned goat is just plain dangerous to have around the homestead. A playful head butt can end in serious injury.

Making Peace

Address issues before they arise by chatting with the neighbors before you bring home a pair of goats. Reassure them that foul odors and noise will not be a major issue. Tell them that goats are generally not noisy creatures and you plan to keep their living quarters clean and well-maintained. Plus, you can tempt neighbors with yummy homemade goat cheese—which is much cheaper than store-bought!

You may be surprised to find that talking to neighbors about your latest ventures into urban homesteading strengthens your relationship. Often people are pleased they were considered and kept in the loop. Opening up clear lines of communication on farm animals can lead to other lines of communication: sharing stories about Grandma's farm, exchanging recipes, and inviting neighborhood kids over to pet the goats.

Housing

A goat house is essential so the goats can escape rain, snow, strong winds, and hot sun. It doesn't need to be fancy, but it's going to most likely be a visible part of your backyard, so get creative with paint and materials. A cob goat house could be a fun project that creates an amazing centerpiece in the backyard homestead.

Ultimately, the structure needs to have at least three sides, or four sides if one side is used as a door. The roof should be angled, as goats love to climb and explore, which can wear out the structure faster. (The roof was the favorite hangout spot for a goat that used to live in my neighborhood.) The floor can be dirt, provided it is well-drained and kept dry.

The door or opening to the house should face south so the sun can warm the interior. It should also allow good ventilation to keep the air fresh and prevent moisture from building up, which can lead to bacteria and mold issues. Avoid drafts, which can make the goats uncomfortable and susceptible to illness.

Goats are happiest if the temperature stays around 55 to 70 degrees Fahrenheit, although they can tolerate temps between 0 and 80 degrees. They have a harder time with hot weather than cold, so they may hang out in the shade or in the goat house when it gets too hot in the sun. Consider temporarily moving the goats into a more-insulated space like a barn or the garage until the weather improves if you live an area with extreme cold and temperatures dropping below zero.

The goat house should allow roughly fifteen square feet per standard goat or ten square feet for miniature goats. It would be convenient for the goat house to include an additional secure area to store feed, bedding, and other supplies. Emphasis should be placed on *secure*. Curious goats that discover where the food is kept will relentlessly try to get back in to gorge themselves as if it's a twenty-four-hour buffet. If you are tight on space, build a house just big enough for the goats to hang out in and use another space, like a garage, for storing supplies.

In addition to the goat house, they need a large yard to roam around in for

exercise. Locate the yard just south of the goat house so the sun can warm the area and keep it dry. It's important that the yard, in addition to the goat house, have good drainage to prevent hoof problems and maintain sanitary conditions.

The fencing around the yard needs to be incredibly sturdy. Goats are well-known to be both curious and agile, often knocking down weak fences or climbing over them. The fence should be at least five feet in height for standard goats, four feet for miniatures. You may even want to consult fellow goatkeepers or talk to the farm supply store to get recommendations on fencing material and whether electric fencing may be a good option.

Dairy goats also need a place for regular milking. Often called the milk parlor, this area should be separate from the goat house and yard to maintain a very high level of cleanliness. It helps if the milk parlor has plumbing installed and a concrete floor so everything can be sprayed down after milking. Some people have made this work by converting the garage or mudroom to suit milking purposes. Wherever the milk parlor ends up being located, it needs to be a large enough space to accommodate a cabinet full of milking supplies, the milk stand, and a sink—and you and the goat, of course.

Supplies

A few basic supplies are necessary to keep happy and healthy goats, plus a few more for milking purposes.

A manger, which is the feeding trough, will need to be purchased or built so the goats' food is raised off the ground. They are messy eaters, so they drop just about as much as they eat. You can avoid wasting food by using a keyhole manger. They have slits on the sides for the goats to slip their heads in and reach the food without pulling things out and onto the ground. You need one keyhole per goat, plus additional ones for salt and baking soda.

Goats are messy eaters, but a manger will prevent food from spilling out.

Clean water needs to be available at all times to your goat herd. After all, milk is approximately 87 percent water! Goats need water to help digestion, increase milk production, process nutrients, and control body temperature. If they go without, it can pose a serious danger to their health.

Keeping goats is a weighty enterprise, so plan to invest in some items to make your life easier. For example, have the goat house and yard wired for both electricity and plumbing. Electricity is needed so you can place the goats' water on a warmer if and when the temperature drops below freezing. Plumbing makes your life easier because you can install an automatic waterer that refills as the goats drink. Saving time here eases the responsibility burden of milking duties.

High-quality legume hay, like alfalfa, helps goats replace nutrients lost in milking. They can eat as much as 3 percent of their body weight a day in just hay. Milkers need to be fed a feed mixture in addition to hay in order to achieve adequate nutrition levels. Beginning homesteaders should buy commercial feed mixtures intended for dairy goats, often referred to as concentrate. They are typically a mix of grains that are whole, cracked, and rolled. The blend offers the correct amount of protein to balance what they eat in roughage, or hay. Plan to feed milking does $1/2$ pound of concentrate for every pound of milk they are producing, decreasing the amount as their milk production declines.

Milk goats also need salt and baking soda in addition to high-quality hay and feed. Does will lose a little salt when they produce milk. Provide mineralized salt in loose form, rather than a block, in one of the manger keyholes. They will self-regulate by eating it when they need to replenish their salt levels.

Baking soda, or sodium bicarbonate, is needed to maintain the proper rumen pH level. This allows them to absorb nutrients, and it also prevents digestive problems. Keep it accessible in one of the keyholes on the manger.

The milk parlor needs to include a milk stand, an elevated platform where your does stand while you sit on a stool below them. The stand should be somewhere around fifteen to eighteen inches in height, depending on what a comfortable height is for you. It helps to have a

Goats must be kept in pairs or more, otherwise they become lonely and depressed.

keyhole stanchion at one end so the does can munch on grain as a distraction from the milking. The stand should be located right where the goats enter the milk parlor. This will make it that much easier to train them to jump up on the stand immediately after entering.

The milk parlor should also include a cabinet to keep milking supplies, which include a scale, baby wipes, dishwashing soap, bleach for cleaning, a milk pail, storage containers, a funnel, and a cup for the first few milk squirts. There should be a shelf for smaller supplies as well, like bag balm, teat dip, and dairy acid cleaner.

The cost of feeding a goat varies, but start by planning about $1 per day per goat. Then do some research on prices at your feed store to get a firmer estimate, since costs vary by region and accessibility to supplies. The start-up cost for initial supplies like milking equipment, mangers, and strong fencing can add up to be a hefty amount. All of these costs reflect the serious commitment to raising happy dairy goats, making other livestock like chickens and ducks seem very simple and cheap in comparison. Keeping a couple dwarf goats on the modern homestead does need to be thought through carefully, but it's a decision that can be incredibly rewarding, providing a constant supply of lip-smacking milk.

Choosing Breeds

There are more than eighty goat breeds worldwide, but only a few are used for milking. Milking breeds produce more milk than their kids need, and they produce it long after kids are weaned. Choose breeds specifically for milking, as the others will be too unproductive to be worth the effort.

Typically you can choose from six standard milk goat breeds in the United States: Nubian, Saanen, French Alpine, Oberhasli, Toggenburg, and La Mancha. Standard goats weigh an average of 130 to 170 pounds, depending on the breed, and males are often larger than females. Here are some general breed characteristics:

- **Nubian:** The most popular breed of milk goat, Nubians have Roman noses, long droopy ears, and produce slightly less milk that has a high butterfat content.
- **Saanen:** The second most popular breed, these are large goats that are all white with pointy ears. They generally have a very high milk production rate.
- **French Alpine:** These goats' coloration can vary from white to black and mixtures in between. This breed has the highest production rate of the milk breeds.
- **Oberhasli:** This is a less common breed in the United States, previously called Swiss Alpine. They are a reddish brown color with black markings. Milk production varies.
- **Toggenburg:** The second highest producer of milk behind the French Alpines, this goat breed is often brown with white accents on either side of the tail, face, and underside of legs.
- **La Mancha:** This breed's most notable characteristic is its tiny ears. They are said to have a good temperament and are very productive.

As mentioned earlier, miniature goats are an excellent alternative for the urban dweller. They take up less valuable space in the backyard and can still produce an ample supply of milk for the family. Miniature goats are also much easier to handle and transport.

The two major miniature goat breeds are the Nigerian Dwarf and the African Pygmy. Both are very good milk producers on average. Their milk is often sweeter than standard goats', meaning it is higher in butterfat. Here are more details:

- **Nigerian Dwarf:** This breed is technically a dual-purpose, meat-milk goat and the most popular breed for the urban goatkeeper. They were popular for a time as pets, so be sure you are buying goats bred for milking. It is very difficult to train a goat out of bad behavior habits. These goats average seventy-five pounds in weight, with females getting about eighteen inches tall and males twenty inches.
- **African Pygmy:** This breed is slightly smaller than the Nigerian Dwarf, with does weighing an average of fifty-five pounds and ranging in height from sixteen to twenty-three inches. They have a stocky appearance and produce milk with very high butterfat content.

You do not necessarily need purebred milking goats, which are often used for showing. So you may end up buying a less expensive, but still productive, grade milk goats. That means one parent was a purebred and the other was unknown or a mixed breed. That is not necessarily a bad thing, as long as the goats were bred together for good milk production.

Obtaining Goats

Goats are most often purchased through farms directly when the goats are young, or at any age through classified ads, both online and in the newspaper. It is important to be selective when acquiring dairy goats. You will want to review their milk records to get a sense of how productive they are if they are already milking. Look at the milk records of their mother to see what kind of parentage they are coming from if you are raising the goats yourself.

Healthy goats should be energetic, curious, and clean. Take a look around at their living conditions to ensure the goats are coming from a responsible owner. Taking careful note of the animals' overall condition and living quarters will increase your chances of acquiring goats in solid condition.

You can begin your milking adventures with backyard goats by buying kids, a dry doe, or a currently milking doe. Buying a kid is the most complicated way to start a herd of milk goats, but also the cheapest. The dry doe is a little less complicated, but the already-milking doe is by far the easiest.

Only buy kids when you can inspect the mother and her milking records. Buying a kid is a gamble, since you won't know how much milk the kid will eventually produce, but you can get an idea by getting to know her mother's history. A baby goat is cute, but you will need to wait until she can have a kid of her own before she will produce milk. That involves feeding her for several months before she is old enough to mate. It also involves finding a buck to mate her with. She will also need to be trained for the milk stand before she gives birth. This can all be a long, somewhat complicated process.

When buying a dry doe, you want to avoid one that was dried up on purpose to sell because she was a bad milker. Carefully inspect her previous milking records and find out exactly why her current owners are selling her. A doe that has been recently bred will be your best bet, because you know she is fertile if you need to breed her again in two to three years. She will cost a little more, but it can be worth the security of her being fertile.

Insist on getting a written guarantee of a doe's pregnancy before buying her. If the buck is registered, also get a service memo prior to purchasing the doe or any money exchanging hands. This will make future kids more valuable because they can be fully registered with a proven lineage.

The easiest entry into keeping milk goats is to buy a doe, or two, who are already milking. They will be used to the milking process, and perhaps you can tailor your routine to match the previous owners' so they transition smoothly. They are the most expensive, but you can look at their milking records to be sure they will be a great backyard addition to your homestead.

Milking

Ask someone how much milk you can expect from the average goat and you will have a difficult time getting an answer. This is due to the wide fluctuation in production based on breed, age, health conditions, parentage, and so on. You can expect an average of 1,800 pounds or 900 quarts of milk a year per standard goat if you did careful research when acquiring your dairy goats to make sure they are good milkers.

That is a whole lot of milk for the modern homesteader, which is another reason why miniature goats may be a wiser choice. Pygmies and dwarves produce relatively similar amounts of milk, roughly 600 pounds or 300 quarts a year. (The recipes in chapter four show you how to turn all that milk into delicious cheese!)

The two most important factors when it comes to milking are cleanliness and keeping the animals calm. The process runs much smoother with a chilled-out doe. It helps to talk or even sing to the ladies while you milk. Often people use this as an opportunity to feed the girls their daily ration of grain. It is another way to keep them occupied while you get down to business.

Goats get used to routine and structure; in fact, they prefer it. Begin the milking routine with the leader of the herd and work your way down the hierarchy. They will get used to knowing when it's their turn on the milking stand, which keeps them calm and collected. They should be milked as close to twelve hours apart as possible.

Before you start milking, brush your goat down to prevent hair and dirt from falling into the milk pail. After brushing her down, clean her udders with baby wipes or a clean, soapy washcloth. The first couple sprays of milk should go into a separate cup and be checked for signs of illness, then tossed out. Gently squeeze the teats (yes, as a goatkeeper you need to start using the term *teats*), alternating between the two, into the milk pail, being careful to not pull on them. When the milk begins to taper off, try massaging the udders to see if more milk comes. When you are all done, use a little teat dip specifically made for goats to ensure bacteria cannot enter the openings.

Milk is highly perishable and should be cooled quickly and immediately after milking. Never add warm milk to already cooled milk. Put the milk in the fridge before cleaning everything up.

Milk supplies should be thoroughly cleaned after each use to reduce the risk of bacteria growth. Scrub everything with a stiffly bristled brush under warm water first, which helps any milk fat come off. Then clean everything again in hot water with dishwashing soap and a dash of bleach. Rinse thoroughly, dip in dairy acid cleaner, then rinse once more before putting safely back into the supply cabinet.

If your goat has never been milked before, get her used to getting up on the milking stand by bribing her with a bit of grain. Do this every day at the same time so she learns the drill. While she is on the milk stand, brush her and wash her teats as part of the routine. Gradually increase the amount of time she is on the stand and the amount of grain you are feeding her as you start milking her.

Once she has her first kid, give her four or five days off so her baby can drink the colostrum the momma is producing. Start the separation process after this time by locking the goats up separately at night, but within sight or smell distance. The first night will be the hardest, but it gets easier over time. When you pick up the routine again of putting the doe on the milk stand, she should know the drill already, which makes the milking process easier.

Health and Safety

In addition to regular milking, goats require some ongoing maintenance. Hooves have to be periodically trimmed,

Singing to your doe will relax her during milking.

which is best done on the milking stand. Testing a goat's milk from the first couple squirts will also allow you to spot health problems early.

Their rumen should also be closely monitored to make sure it's working properly. A rumen is the first compartment in the stomach where food is stored before being returned back to the mouth for the animal to chew. Cows, bison, and gazelles are all members of the ruminant family. Chewing cud and burping are signs that the rumen is in good shape. You can also see the occasional ripple across goats' left side, in an upward motion, that shows the rumen is working.

Goats benefit from exercise out in the goat yard. Give them some large boulders to climb on or build them some platforms for climbing and playing. Train miniature goats early on a dog harness and try going on walks on local trails. They will enjoy being new places and munching on an even wider variety of plants during the walk. Just mind that they don't make a beeline for the neighbor's roses.

Find a good veterinarian who has experience caring for goats. You will want someone trustworthy and knowledgeable to call if ever serious health issues arise. It is quite common to go an entire backyard-poultry-keeping lifetime without ever calling the vet, but goats are more complicated animals. It's always better to be too prepared than too little prepared.

Goatsitting

Goats are intelligent animals that need supervision, which means there is a far greater responsibility to find a reliable goatsitter when you go on vacation. Even if you decide to take a day trip somewhere, you need to make sure they get milked every twelve hours. Set up a network of reliable people who can lend a hand when you need help.

Online communities are popping up all the time for modern homesteaders who keep backyard goats. Get connected early to tap into local resources for potential help watching over your herd. Start making friends at the feed store with other resident goatkeepers. Perhaps you can hire people with a herd of their own to stop by and perform milking duties. Or maybe you can swap goatsitting and watch their herd the next time they go on vacation.

Consider training a good friend or family member on how to care for a small herd of goats. It may work out easiest to have him or her stay at your house while you are out of town. The goatsitter will need to sit in on a milking with you to understand the order in which the does are milked and the details of the milking process. Write down careful notes for your goatsitter, since there is a lot to remember. Include all necessary emergency numbers. Your sitter will also need to clean out the bedding if you plan to be gone for several days.

Set up a nice guest room, stock the fridge with delicious goat cheese, and bring home an expensive bottle of wine to thank your goatsitter for helping you out. Doing this well in advance of booking your vacation will ensure you and your herd have a relaxing vacation.

THE BEE'S KNEES

Bees are fascinating, productive creatures that can easily fit into the modern homestead. They require little in the way of a living space, which is the hive, and will travel all around the neighborhood collecting pollen. In fact, growing numbers of urbanites are keeping hives on rooftops in densely crowded cities like New York in order to have access to delicious, homegrown honey. The stacks of colorful wooden bee boxes can be a playful addition outside, and multiple hives can fit comfortably in the same backyard, patio, or rooftop. Each hive can produce over a hundred pounds of honey every year.

There are numerous benefits to keeping your own colony of honeybees. The most obvious one is that you'll have a very large source of honey made right on the premises. The comb, a by-product from the colony, can be melted down and used for various crafts, like candle-making, or in beauty products, like hand salves. Nearby fruit trees and shrubs will all benefit with increased fruit yields due to the higher pollination rates from your bees. And, best of all from an environmentalist's perspective, you will be supporting the local bee population by providing additional habitat.

A love of nature and a love of puttering is a good personality fit for keeping bees. Use your imagination on where to situate the hive, because a yard is not required. Luckily, the increasing popularity of urban homesteading has led to an increase in introductory beekeeping workshops through garden centers and community garden clubs. Typically these workshops are in the spring, which is the ideal time to start a hive.

The more you learn about keeping bees, the more you discover there is to learn. There is no one way to do something right, but here is one perspective on how to keep a successful hive.

A wooden bee box fits into a small corner of the homestead.

Bees 101

There are more than 20,000 species of bees, but only seven are honeybees. There are no honeybees native to North America, so honeybees in the United States were actually brought in from Europe and Africa.

A bee colony can accommodate anywhere from 15,000 to 100,000 individual bees. The population will reach its peak at the height of the pollen season, usually midsummer, and drop through the winter months. Each colony has its own unique temperament: calm, aggressive/mean, curious. If the colony is too aggressive, some beekeepers purposely kill the queen and carefully introduce a new queen. It's up to the individual queen to set the tone of the colony.

Within a colony, bees fall into three different categories, each with its own set of responsibilities. They are the queen, female workers, and male drones. The most revered member of the colony is the queen.

There is only one queen bee in a colony. She is much larger than the female worker bees and longer in shape than the drones. She is typically the only reproducing female in the colony, laying up to 1,500 eggs per day and approximately 350,000 eggs per year. She can live up to age five and is typically replaced her second year.

It takes several days after the queen is born for her to be able to fly. Often the queen has poor eyesight and is not a very good flyer. She will embark on what is referred to as her virgin flight when the temperature reaches about 70 degrees Fahrenheit. This is the only time she leaves the colony. She will visit a nearby drone congregation area (DCA) and mate with up to twenty drone bees—what a free-lovin' swinger! She stores the sperm for her entire life, which she uses to produce female worker bee eggs. No sperm is required to make male drones.

Worker bees are all female but are smaller in size than the queen. They represent about 99 percent of the colony and work for the hive as nurse, house, and field/forager bees.

- **Nurse bees:** These bees are between the ages of one and twelve days old. They are in charge of cleaning out cells where eggs are hatched and feeding the eggs.
- **House bees:** These bees are ten to twenty days old and are responsible for building comb, removing the queen feces (everyone else goes outside the hive to defecate), removing dead bees, guarding the hive, controlling the climate by shivering to generate heat, and accepting pollen and nectar from the forager bees.
- **Field/Forager bees:** These bees are over twenty days old, living somewhere from thirty to forty-five days total. They are the bees we see most often, as it is their job to collect nectar in the form of pollen and gather water and plant resins.

All male bees are drones, which represent less than 1 percent of the colony's total population. These poor boys are only good for one thing and get kicked out of the hive in the fall, when they are no longer needed for reproduction. They also die after mating. Sorry, dudes!

Nate wears protective clothing that reduces bee stings but still breathes.

In the spring, the bee colony population needs to increase so bees can stock up on honey to get through the next winter. A small number of hatching bees will be drones while the rest will be worker bees. Every couple years, a new queen is born and takes over the colony.

The female worker bees determine when it is time to hatch a new queen bee, more worker bees, or drone bees. Talk about power to the people! The worker bees are the ones who prepare the cells (areas in the comb where eggs are laid), and what the queen bee lays is based on the cell size. The queen feels with her antennae to determine if it is a big cell or small cell. She lays an unfertilized egg to become a drone if it is a big cell. When the cell is small, she will lay a fertilized egg that will become a worker bee.

The worker bees are also in charge of managing the overall population of the colony. They single out one cell to house the next queen bee when they determine it is time for someone new to take the throne. They build the cell into a peanut shape so it is much larger than any other cell. The current queen comes along and lays a regular female egg in the large cell. The workers then feed the future queen larva royal jelly to build up her strength. The new queen is hatched in only sixteen days, where worker bees need twenty-one days and drones need twenty-four days to develop.

Making Peace

Many cities allow beekeeping, and several require a permit. In my experience, most urban beekeepers I have met fly under the radar without a permit. Legislation changes often, so check with your local extension office to find out more details about the current policy where you live.

Once you have established the legality of keeping bees on your homestead, be a good neighbor and talk to those living close by. Bees are docile creatures that prefer to be left to themselves and their work. They will likely increase the pollination of nearby trees and shrubs, which should give your neighbors heavier crops.

But begin your adventures into beekeeping with an open line of communication with your neighbors. The occasional jars of honey or homemade candles can go a long way in winning allies.

A word of caution about water: bees are attracted to nearby water sources. If someone has a swimming pool or pond nearby, they very well might discover you have bees on their own. Don't let them find out the hard way when they notice a hundred bees lounging poolside. Take early steps when establishing your new hive to train bees to a nearby water source in your own yard. This will reduce the chance that they make a habit of hanging out at the neighbor's pool.

Ensure there are no openings in your clothing when harvesting honey.

Housing

There are a number of ways to set up your home-scale bee operation, and chances are everyone you ask will have his own opinion on the matter. Beekeeping is as interesting and eclectic as beekeepers themselves.

Backyard bees need to be kept in hive boxes, which can either be homemade or purchased. Although you can build your own hive, I recommend buying new equipment when you are starting out. If you find used equipment, ensure it has not been used by diseased bees. Hive boxes and other beekeeping equipment can be purchased through mail-order catalogs or specialized beekeeping shops. You may even get lucky and find supplies at the local farm and feed store, so do some scouting.

You should begin with two deep boxes often referred to as brood boxes. This is where the majority of the colony will live. There are a few different size options for brood boxes, but I recommend the deep $9\,^5/_8$-inch ones, which can weigh up to eighty or ninety pounds when filled with honey. You don't harvest from this box, though, as this is the permanent dwelling for the bees. The honey they fill these two boxes with will feed them through the long winter months.

A super is an additional box you place on top of the brood boxes that the bees fill with excess honey. The bees will not live in these boxes, as they have enough room down below in the two large brood boxes. The supers are smaller and easier to manage when harvesting honey. As one fills up, simply add a new one on top, creating a tall stack. Eventually you could have two brood boxes stacked with one to five supers on top. Choose western-style super boxes, which are $6\,^1/_4$ inches deep.

If you have some experience with bees or have an experienced friend helping you assemble boxes, always use both glue and nails. Boxes get very heavy when filled with honey. My grandpa would always advise using both glue and nails to ensure a strong build on almost any construction project, and that holds especially true in this scenario.

Colonies need to stay dry, otherwise the bees can get too cold and die off. Position the hive boxes where they will get some sun. It's ideal if the hive is situated in a place sheltered from strong winds. It's easiest to harvest the honey from the side of the hive, so keep access open on either side. Take extra time to make sure you have a good spot. It is difficult to move the hive much farther than 2 feet at a time once bees get established.

Provide fresh water somewhere near the hive at all times. If you train your bees from the beginning to access this spot for water, it will make things much easier. Keep in mind that bees are not good swimmers, so put rocks in the source, for example a birdbath, so they can access the water without drowning. A small moss garden can be both attractive and a great way to give bees access to water. Just set a collection of various small moss pots into a large tray and water often.

Supplies

I recommend you buy a full-body harvesting suit to prevent stings from the bees—you *will* most definitely get stung at some point. Although they can be mellow creatures, bees will start to become stressed in late summer when there are fewer pollen sources. They may be more apt to sting when you are out there harvesting honey.

Gloves are also highly recommended and come with insets either of netting or solid cloth. Every beekeeper has her preference of equipment, but I prefer the gloves with solid cloth. Bees can easily be sitting on the netting when you move your hands, squish them, and get a sting. Still, it's a hot business being out in the summer sunshine unloading super boxes weighted down with honey. Netting can be desirable for air circulation, but at least you know the trade-off is a greater possibility of stings.

A queen excluder is something you place between the two brood boxes and the supers on top, which are intended for excess honey. The queen, being larger, cannot fit through the excluder, but the worker bees can. First, let the worker bees draw out the supers, meaning let them make cells/comb ready for eggs. Then insert the excluder so the queen can't go up there to lay eggs.

The benefit of the excluder is that now the queen will stay safely in the bottom two brood boxes. The worst thing you could do when harvesting honey is slide a frame back into place and accidentally squish the queen, eventually killing your colony. With her safely in the bottom box, she can keep laying eggs while the excess honey can keep filling the upper super boxes.

Good gloves and a head covering make harvesting relatively painless.

Obtaining Bees and Breed Selection

There are stories about "build it and they will come" when someone gets her hive boxes all set up and a random swarm just moves in overnight. Some laugh off this idea, while others swear by it. In general, you should obtain your bees by mail-order catalogs, through specialty bee shops, or by capturing a swarm. Do not attempt to capture a swarm on your own, rather take this as an opportunity to make some new friends.

Call your local beekeeping association and let them know you are interested in starting a new hive. You may have to pay a fee, but they can often let you know the next time they get a frantic call from someone with a bee colony living in their chimney. The beekeepers can catch the swarm and hopefully bring it to you for a fee.

If you decide to purchase bees by catalog or from a specialty shop, you may get to choose the breed yourself. Take their advice on the best beginner bee suited to your climate. Some are better at over-wintering than others.

If the decision is entirely up to you, choose the Italian honeybee. It is generally considered to be a great general-purpose bee. They quickly build comb, make great foragers, keep the hive quite clean, and are relatively calm in demeanor.

Swarming

It is not fully understood why colonies swarm, but it can often be attributed to overcrowding. A colony is unlikely to swarm in the first year. In preparation for swarming, worker bees keep the queen moving so she sheds some weight for the big flight, resulting in no eggs being laid.

Bees typically swarm within 100 feet of the colony, where they remain for anywhere from twenty minutes to two weeks. During that time, scouts are sent out in different directions to find a new permanent home.

The bees are less likely to sting while they are swarming because the worker bees gorged themselves before flight, not knowing when their next meal would be. A bee needs to bend its stinger down to sting, which is painful with a full stomach.

It is not recommended for beginner beekeepers to capture a swarm, so enlist the help of an expert. Most areas have a "swarm hotline" that is operated by the local beekeeping association. When capturing a swarm, it is often easiest to cut off the branch they are swarming onto and shake them into a bee box. I have seen them swarm onto the side of a building, though, in the windowsill area. In that case, the bee people gently swept the bees off the building and into a hive box.

About 80 percent of the colony can reasonably be expected to be captured, sometimes less, and the box should be left out overnight near the swarming location. The other 20 percent will eventually return when they intercept the pheromones from the other colony members, which alert them to the new colony location in the box.

Harvesting

The highest honey production months are those with the highest pollen count. In the Northern Hemisphere, this will often be the months of June and July, when everything in town is blooming.

Before you begin harvesting honey, take off all of the supers. Add an empty super with a trap screen and stack the full supers on top. You now have two brood boxes, an empty super, a trap screen, and full supers on top. As the worker bees go down from the full supers into the brood boxes to check in with the colony, they cannot move back up through the trap screen.

It will take about a day for all the bees to move out of the full supers. Once they have made their way out of the full supers, you can harvest without disturbing the bees as much. You can add a couple new supers and remove the trap screen, allowing them to keep busy filling the empty supers with honey. This also gives you plenty of time to let the honey drain out of the full supers.

Harvesting honey is one sticky business. You may end up with two or three full supers sitting in the kitchen, extracting the honey by hand with a scraper into big buckets...and all the while the bees are outside filling up new supers.

At the end of the summer, all of the supers come off. The honey season is over and it's time for the bees to be done

Bees actively collect pollen on a warm, sunny afternoon.

working. They will stay inside the hive most of the time to wait out the cold weather and eat their honey stores.

Honey can be used in place of sugar in baking and cooking or it can be used in beauty products. Chapter four includes recipes to help you use your excess honey in cold elixirs, appetizers, face masks, and hand salves. Honey does not go bad, so store it for use all winter long.

Health and Safety

Freeze your supers for twenty-four hours before winter storage to cut down on disease. This will kill any wax moth larvae and other pests. Clean 20 to 30 percent of your frames each year to keep disease down and prevent old cells from getting too narrow.

A screened bottom board, instead of solid wood, can be left on the brood box year-round. It will not create a strong draft since it's on the bottom of the hive stack, but it does allow some good ventilation. When mites attach themselves to the bees, they will fall off and out of the tray, instead of onto a solid floor still within the hive. Try to ensure there are never openings on opposite sides of the boxes for entering and exiting, as this will create a draft running through the colony.

The bee colony population will decline naturally in the winter because the colony doesn't need as many worker bees when there is less pollen to harvest. The hive could be 80,000 strong in the summer, with only 15,000 overwintering at minimum. The brood boxes may get light in the winter, which means the bees have eaten all of their stored honey.

Place an upside-down jar filled with two parts sugar and one part water into the hive in winter. The bees will live off this syrup when the honey is getting pretty light. Punch very small holes in the lid of the jar so water doesn't drip out but the bees can drink. This isn't always necessary, but it's important to keep an eye on your bees in the winter months in case they need the assistance.

Beesitting

Bees are independent creatures that will come and go on their own, without much attention from you. In fact, the less you interfere with them, the happier they'll be going about their daily work.

Aside from a friend stopping by the homestead once a week to make sure the hive hasn't been knocked over by a fallen tree limb, there is not much need of any beesitting while you are out of town. Enjoy your vacation and rest assured they are happily building stores of honey in your absence.

WINTER'S COMING

Unlike our garden spaces, which we can put to bed in the fall, animals are a year-round commitment and responsibility. Wildlife might hibernate or migrate south in the winter, but livestock are still alive and bustling in the cold months of the year. As the days get shorter, there are some ways to prepare your animals for the winter.

Consider doing an annual deep cleaning of the poultry or goat housing on a dry, sunny fall day. White vinegar is a natural, nontoxic disinfectant that can kill molds, bacteria, and unwanted germs. I scrub it into the walls, floors, and other surfaces to ensure it gets into the nooks and crannies. Once it has dried, hose everything off and allow it to air dry thoroughly.

Carefully store the unneeded supers and screens from your beehive in a place protected from moisture and extreme cold. Spend a little extra time organizing supplies so they are easy to access in early spring. Keep a careful eye on the colony through the winter to determine when they are running out of honey and in need of supplemental sugar water.

Stock up on livestock supplies like feed, bedding, and supplies while the weather is still decent. Hauling bales of straw and hay in winter rain, snow, or ice can be a real drag. Having these supplies on hand will spare you the hassle of running to and from the feed store on cold, dark evenings.

Look your animals over carefully in the fall and spring. Check that they are clean, healthy, and pest free. You may not be outside as often peeking in on them, so you want to enter the winter knowing they are all in the best of health.

Chapter Four
PRESERVING THE HARVEST

One of the greatest rewards from my homesteading efforts is seeing my shelves stocked with homemade sauces, the freezer packed with frozen produce, and a caddy of green household cleaners made from scratch sitting in my pantry. Summer afternoons spent preserving the harvest are calm, reflective times that become some of my most savored memories of the year. A typical scene includes Bob Dylan humming on my vintage record player while the kitchen fills up with savory smells that linger all evening. Every jar I add to the shelf turns into a new wave of self-sufficient empowerment.

This ritual of preserving food has been going on for thousands and thousands of years as a practical way to stretch the

A well-stocked cupboard stretches the harvest.

One can never have too many jars of berry preserves.

Anytime the economy takes a tumble, we once more look to food preservation for affordable and nutritious options.

Today food is preserved for several reasons. Preserving your own homegrown, organic produce is a cost-effective way to get high-quality food all year. I was fortunate to grow up with a pantry stocked with homemade goods, and our families today deserve the same access to safe and healthy food. It is better for the environment to source food close to home. The overall quality of the food you eat at home also increases significantly when it comes from your own backyard or your favorite local farm, especially in the winter months when few fresh vegetables and fruits are in season.

Whether I am making the most of my harvest by cooking in season or preserving it for the winter, it gives me a self-reliant sense of accomplishment that I am doing my part for the environment and my well-being. I try every year to preserve enough excess produce to get me through to the next gardening season, plus extras to give away as homemade gifts. Friends come over for canning parties, which allow us to hang out and be productive at the same time.

Tie on an apron, put on some tunes, and start stocking the cupboards with food you can boast about all winter long.

Cooking Fresh
Means Cooking Seasonally

Cooking with fresh produce is by far the best way to enjoy the rich flavors that nature created. No vegetable, fruit, egg,

harvest. Perhaps one of the earliest preservation methods was drying—someone left an uneaten piece of fruit out in the hot sun. They found it was lighter to carry around and was still edible weeks later. According to the National Center for Home Food Preservation, Middle Eastern cultures were drying foods way back in 12,000 BC. Preserving foods freed humans up to settle down somewhere and take a break from the constant search for food.

For Americans, food preservation became wildly popular out of necessity during the Great Depression. A few years later, World War II hit and thousands of Americans preserved the harvest to free up food supplies for the troops abroad.

milk, or even meat, for that matter, is better tasting than when it is freshly picked or processed. A tomato never tastes as delicious as when you bite into one freshly picked from your garden. It's magical and it makes all your homesteading trials and tribulations worth it in just one bite.

In order to make the most of your harvest, you need to learn to cook seasonally. That can be a huge mind-set adjustment, especially if you didn't grow up around a garden or farm, or if you aren't a frequent customer at farmers' markets. Admittedly, my first couple seasons of homesteading left me with piles of food I didn't know what to do with. My neighbors received many bowls of free eggs, and too much garden produce ended up in the compost bin because I just couldn't use it all fast enough. At least it went to use

Fall means winter squash for breakfast, lunch, and dinner.

somewhere, but I would have preferred to make it useful in my belly.

The concept of eating seasonally is relatively straightforward: we structure our meals around what is currently growing and producing. This includes all the herbs, vegetables, fruits, eggs, milk, and meat produced on our homesteads. The main ingredients in our meals are planned around what we have and are then rounded out with foods we've preserved or purchased at the store. "What's for dinner?" gets answered by "What's in season?" Learning to cook in season is something much easier said than done, though, and it can take some practice to figure out what is grown when.

To complicate things, what is growing in California in January will be very different from what is growing in New York at the same time of year. You need to discover the seasonality of food crops in your specific neck of the woods. A valuable resource in learning to determine the seasonality of local food is to check out your local farmers' market. You will start to notice trends at the market stand and in your backyard, which eventually makes is easier for you to anticipate what should be featured on next week's menu.

There are a few tricks to making it easier to eat fresh as the garden is harvested: stockpile recipes, shop at home first, and plan meals in advance.

Stockpiling recipes means you need to comb the Internet, flip through cookbooks, and trade recipes with friends that call for things you are tending on your homestead. If you want to grow kale but are not used to cooking with it, try to gather three or four recipes that sound tasty and require a glut of kale. If you are ready to keep ducks, talk to friends and farmers who keep ducks so you can use some of their favorite recipes.

When all else fails, try an easy cooking method of steaming, roasting, or sautéing any given vegetable and serve it as a side dish that week for dinner. Lightly season it with olive oil, salt, and pepper and enjoy the taste of simplicity. Take note when you find a good taste combination, like kale with bacon, chard with a dash of maple syrup, broccoli with extra-sharp cheddar cheese, zucchini with lemon juice, and tomatoes with basil.

The idea of shopping at home first means that you take a look at what you have at home before buying food from the grocery store. Take an inventory of what you have growing, what canned goods you preserved, what dried foods are in the cupboard, and what you have frozen. To make this process quicker, keep a master list on the fridge. Write down every can of marinara sauce you preserve or bag of peas you freeze. As the year goes on, check things off the list when they are used. When you do finally visit the grocery store, you are just picking up smaller ingredients to round out a recipe.

It's not the end of the world if a broccoli goes to seed before you end up eating it, or if you just can't keep up with the storm of zucchini. Composting the waste means it will still work toward building up next year's garden. And

don't be shy about trading with friends! It's a great idea to swap food throughout the season—a few logs of goat cheese in exchange for jars of honey, for example. It gives you a break from something you've been eating for weeks, and someone else gets to enjoy something new.

Brussels sprouts are worth the wait. Snip off larger buds as needed during colder months.

Recipes

Embracing the farm-to-table approach, here are some lively, tasty recipes for a munchy snack, a quick lunch, or an elegant dinner party. Whether the table is gussied up or not, you'll still be glowing with pride knowing your hard work is deliciously paying off. *Bon appétit!*

Zucchini Parmigiana

- 6 zucchini, yellow summer squash, or pattypan squash (or a combo of all three)
- 3 eggs, beaten
- 3 cups breadcrumbs
- 1 tablespoon minced fresh basil
- 1 tablespoon thyme
- 1 clove garlic, minced
- $\frac{1}{2}$ cup olive oil
- 1 cup mozzarella, grated
- $\frac{1}{4}$ cup Parmesan, grated
- 1 quart marinara sauce
- Salt and pepper to taste

1. Preheat oven to 350 degrees Fahrenheit.
2. Slice squash into $\frac{1}{4}$-inch slices lengthwise.
3. Coat squash in beaten egg and roll in breadcrumbs seasoned with the basil, thyme, and garlic.
4. In batches, fry in olive oil on medium heat for about ten minutes on each side. You want them slightly overdone, so it's okay if they get a little black. Add a little more oil for each batch.
5. Arrange a single layer of fried squash evenly in a large casserole. Top with shredded mozzarella and a little Parmesan. Then top with enough marinara sauce to cover.
6. Repeat the previous step until the casserole is full, three to four layers altogether. Sprinkle more cheese on top. I also sprinkle on the remaining breadcrumbs.
7. Bake uncovered for thirty minutes. Check to see how much liquid is in the casserole. If there is a lot of liquid, as the squash purges quite a bit of water, I end up cooking for another thirty minutes. I consider it done when there is liquid only in the bottom quarter of the pan. Let it sit for a few minutes to settle before serving.

Roasted Squash

- $3^1/_2$ pounds butternut squash, peeled and cut into one-inch cubes
- 2 tablespoons minced fresh parsley
- 2 tablespoons olive oil
- 2 garlic cloves, minced
- 1 teaspoon salt
- $^1/_2$ teaspoon pepper
- $^1/_3$ cup grated Parmesan cheese

1. Preheat oven to 400 degrees Fahrenheit.
2. In a large bowl, combine the parsley, oil, garlic, salt, and pepper. Add squash and toss to coat.
3. Transfer to an ungreased, shallow two-quart baking dish. Bake uncovered for fifty to fifty-five minutes or until squash is just tender.

Lemony Kale Chips

- 1 bunch kale
- 2 tablespoons olive oil
- 1 tablespoon balsamic vinegar
- 1 teaspoon lemon juice
- Sea salt and pepper to taste

1. Preheat oven to 400 degrees Fahrenheit.
2. Whisk together oil, vinegar, and lemon juice until well combined. Toss with kale leaves and spread in a single layer on a cookie sheet.
3. Roast in the oven for ten minutes, or until crispy. Sprinkle with salt and pepper to taste.

Maple Greens

- 1 bunch kale, chard, mustard greens, arugula, or a mixture
- 1 tablespoon olive oil
- 1 tablespoon maple syrup

1. Heat oil in a skillet on medium. Add greens and sauté until wilted, about three to five minutes.
2. Add maple syrup and stir until well distributed. Serve warm.

Tomato Salad

- 2 to 3 pounds assorted tomatoes, thickly sliced
- 1 cup loosely packed basil leaves
- $^1/_2$ pound mozzarella, sliced
- $^1/_2$ cup olive oil
- Salt and pepper to taste

1. Alternate layers of tomatoes, basil, and cheese on their sides in a casserole dish. Begin with a tomato slice, then a basil leaf, then a mozzarella slice. Repeat until the serving dish has been filled.
2. Lightly drizzle with olive oil, and add salt and pepper to taste.

German Pancakes

My sister makes these every weekend for brunch and they are fantastic!

- 2 tablespoons butter, melted
- 6 eggs
- 1 cup flour
- 1 cup milk
- $1/2$ teaspoon salt
- $1/4$ cup powdered sugar
- 1 lemon, cut into wedges

1. Preheat oven to 425 degrees Fahrenheit.
2. Melt butter in two 9-inch round cake pans while the oven is warming.
3. Beat the eggs and mix with flour, milk, and salt.
4. Pour mixture into the two pans and bake for fifteen minutes, or until the tops begin to brown.
5. Remove from oven and sprinkle powdered sugar over the pancakes. Squeeze lemon onto the pancakes to taste and enjoy.

Garden Frittata

- 1 tablespoon butter
- 6 eggs
- $1/2$ teaspoon salt
- $1/4$ teaspoon pepper
- $1/2$ cup mozzarella cheese, grated
- $1/4$ cup sun-dried tomatoes, chopped
- $1/4$ cup roasted red bell pepper, chopped
- 2 tablespoons fresh basil, chopped

1. Set oven to broil.
2. Melt butter in a skillet over medium heat.
3. Beat eggs with salt and pepper. Pour egg mixture into skillet.
4. Sprinkle cheese, tomatoes, peppers, and basil over the egg mixture, but do not stir.
5. When eggs begin to set, move the skillet into the oven and finish cooking under the broiler for about five minutes. It will puff up and slightly brown when ready.
6. Remove from oven and enjoy while warm.

Goat Cheese

Making your own goat cheese will help you use up the never-ending supply of fresh milk from your darling ladies, but it can also be made using goats' milk from the grocery store. I used to make this in our teeny New York apartment with local milk purchased from the co-op.

- 1 quart goats' milk, unpasteurized or pasteurized (avoid ultrapasteurized)
- $^1/_4$ cup lemon juice
- Various seasonings

1. Gently heat goats' milk over low-medium heat, stirring occasionally. Use a meat, dairy, or candy thermometer to measure when the milk reaches 180 degrees Fahrenheit. If you don't have a thermometer, heat until just boiling—the milk will be foamy.
2. Remove from heat, add lemon juice, and stir quickly until well combined.
3. After about twenty seconds, pour mixture into a colander that has been lined with many layers of cheesecloth, or line it with a very clean towel.
4. Allow the liquid whey to drain from the cheese, which takes about an hour to an hour and a half. Tie the corners of the cloth together and raise above the colander to drain from all sides.
5. Once the creamy consistency is achieved, salt and season to taste. Try variations like minced garlic with herbes de Provence or cracked black pepper with rosemary. Refrigerate.

Goat Cheese and Roasted Zucchini Sandwiches

This is the perfect homesteader recipe if you have goats in the backyard, zucchini in the garden, and herbs ready to be snipped.

- 2 summer squashes: zucchini, yellow crookneck, etc.
- 2 tablespoons olive oil
- 2 tablespoons minced fresh herbs: lemon balm, thyme, rosemary, basil, etc.
- Salt and pepper to taste
- 4 ounces goat cheese
- Loaf of crusty bread
- 2 tablespoons chives, chopped

1. Preheat oven to 450 degrees Fahrenheit.
2. Brush a short-sided pan with olive oil.
3. Slice summer squashes as thinly as possible, roughly $1/4$ inch lengthwise.
4. Arrange on pan and brush with olive oil.
5. Sprinkle on fresh herbs and generously add salt and pepper.
6. Roast in oven for fifteen minutes.
7. Toast slices of crusty bread.
8. Smear goat cheese on one side of half the toasted bread slices. Top with chives.
9. Pile roasted squash on the other pieces of toasted bread. Pair cheese and squash halves of sandwiches.
10. Devour.

Honey Goat Cheese Dip

- 1 cup plain goat cheese
- $1/2$ cup plain yogurt
- 2 tablespoons honey
- 1 tablespoon mixed minced herbs like sage, thyme, savory, and rosemary

1. Mix all ingredients until well blended.
2. Refrigerate for an hour so flavors marry.
3. Use as a dip for crackers or crusty bread.

Erika's Elixir

My dear friend Erika introduced me to her family's German recipe for *heissezitrone*, which is a wonderful honey tea for when you have a horrible cold. As college roommates, we added a little whiskey to it for a winter nightcap. Save this one if you have bees and an indoor citrus tree.

- 4 cups water
- $1/4$ cup local honey
- 1 teaspoon ginger, grated
- 2 lemons, juiced

1. Heat the water, honey, and ginger together in a small saucepan until boiling.
2. Remove from heat and stir in lemon juice.
3. Drink as a tea to soothe a cold, or add a little whiskey for a winter warm-me-up.

Honey Appetizers

These are some of my favorite pairings for easy appetizers.

- Dried dates stuffed with fresh goat cheese, drizzled with honey.

- Figs sliced in half with a chunk of blue cheese and a dollop of honey in the center.

- Warm honey tossed with mixed nuts, sprinkled lightly with cayenne pepper, and broiled for two to three minutes, watching carefully, until light brown.

Freeze It

There used to be a sign in one of my former office buildings that said "Fast, quality, cheap: pick two." Freezing allows you to pick all three!

Freezing is actually one of the simplest and fastest ways to preserve the harvest. It requires very minimal equipment—something to hold the contents (freezer bags or airtight containers) and a place to put it all (the freezer)—which means it is low cost. Done properly, frozen foods deliver a close-to-fresh taste that you can enjoy months after harvesting. Even if you have an itty-bitty freezer, make room for a couple bags of frozen apples and berries to make into baked goodies.

Pick berries all summer long to encourage them to continue fruiting.

Supplies

Foods stored in the freezer need to be packaged in either plastic freezer bags or rigid containers. When selecting rigid containers for freezing, choose from either plastic or glass. The containers need to make an airtight seal that will keep moisture inside and protect the food from the dry freezer air. Choose containers that have thick walls to prevent cracking once frozen. Regular glass jars will crack, so select ones especially made to tolerate the low temperatures of a freezer.

That said, I reuse plastic food containers from the grocery store all the time for freezing. They have tight-fitting lids, but they are probably not the ideal sealing barrier between food and the freezer. I sometimes get a little freezer burn if the food's in there more than a couple months, but the price can't be beat since the containers were destined for the recycling bin anyway. I have had success with margarine, yogurt, and salsa containers. They are the perfect size for single-serving meals. I just slide the frozen contents into a dinner bowl, heat, and serve.

Freezer bags are an inexpensive and readily available option from the grocery store. They are made with slightly thicker plastic to protect foods from moisture loss and absorbing freezer odors. Reuse them every year by simply washing them with warm, soapy water after use, drying, and storing in a kitchen drawer until needed. Look for sales and stock up so you are never in short supply when you happen to get a glut of something to preserve from the garden.

What to Freeze

Prepare for harvest season by talking to friends, neighbors, and family members who might have an unused fruit tree in their yard. Often they are more than happy to share. My mom, for example, has two dwarf Asian pear trees in her backyard that used to overwhelm her with fruit every year. Instead of making every baked good under the sun and living with the guilt of wasted fruit she can't use in time, she instead calls me and my sister to come collecting.

"99 Luftballons," Kim Carnes's "Bette Davis Eyes," The Cure's "Lovecats," and Michael Jackson's "Billie Jean." We use bags that hold the perfect amount for pies so we can use an entire bag at once. Typically a gallon-sized bag is a close measurement. My mom gets a nice kickback of however many bags she wants as a thank-you for thinking of us.

I generally shop around the farmers' market late in the season for deals on large quantities of produce that I can use throughout the year for cooking. Onions,

Freeze berries in a single layer on a cookie sheet initially, then bag. This prevents them from freezing into a huge clump.

We pick buckets full of the fruit and simply peel, quarter, core, and throw into freezer bags while jamming to 80s music. The mix must include some combination of Madonna's "Like a Prayer," Nena's

bell peppers, carrots, and celery are often used in smaller quantities. Buy them in bulk, peel, and chop them. Then fill a gallon-sized freezer bag with them. Whenever a recipe calls for a little here and there, just reach into the freezer and fill up the measuring cup. It's a very quick and cost-efficient way to stock up from local sources with farming practices I trust.

Tomatoes work well frozen if you plan to cook with them later. They get a little mushy once thawed, but the flavor keeps very well. Before freezing, dip them in boiling water for about thirty seconds until their skins crack. Peel off the skins and core the tops. Think about the quantities you will most likely use in cooking, and place in the most appropriate-sized container. I freeze about two to four cups' worth at a time in smaller bags right when I start

Lemon juice frozen in ice cube trays for use all year.

to feel overwhelmed with too many tomatoes. Most recipes I cook with call for a similar amount, so it works out deliciously.

Freezing berries is an excellent way to preserve their sweet flavor, and they taste almost fresh again when baked into pies and sweets. A tip for freezing berries: spread them out onto a cookie sheet and place the sheet flat in the freezer. Once they have hardened, transfer them into a plastic freezer bag. They will have frozen individually, making it easier to pour some out as needed, as opposed to wrestling with a big solid clump of berries.

Jay and I make a habit of gathering raspberries in the evenings to enjoy over ice cream for dessert. Whatever we don't use gets frozen overnight on the cookie sheet and added to the larger bag of berries the next morning. Delicate berries don't last long once picked, and continual harvesting encourages our plants to produce more fruit.

Snap peas are one of those vegetables that I swear every spring I will never get sick of. But by the time May rolls around, I have eaten enough snap peas to feed a whole army. When you start to feel burned out on a certain veggie, freeze it instead. You can even make a little vegetable medley with green beans, peas, and corn. They all freeze well and provide much-needed vitamins and nutrients during the dark winter months.

When I take trips down South, I check the farmers' markets for citrusy things that don't grow up North. I ride the plane home with a suitcase full of juicy lemons and oranges. After arriving at home, I juice the citrus and pour the juice into ice cube trays. Once they have frozen, I transfer the ice cubes into a freezer container or bag. Throughout the year when a recipe calls for lemon or orange juice, I just reach in and grab a few cubes. It's the next best thing to freshly squeezed!

Purchase meat in bulk from local farmers when it's butchering time. I choose to buy from ranchers who have grass-fed, antibiotic- and hormone-free cattle. Often the meat comes straight from the butcher, packed and wrapped for the freezer in reasonable sizes. If you need to do it yourself, or you happen to get a bulk discount from the local natural grocery store on ground meat, freeze it into either serving sizes or recipe sizes. Freeze ground meat in one-pound increments, since that is the most commonly used size in recipes. Jay and I freeze steaks in increments of two, since we usually cook two at a time.

Most meats, fruits, and vegetables are fine in the freezer, but not everything is meant to be frozen. Things like cheese, eggs, and milk get kind of funky when thawed, so avoid those. Lettuce, cabbage, and cucumbers get really watery and can have an off taste when frozen. Potatoes should also be avoided in the freezer, as they develop a mealy texture when thawed. They are better kept in a cool, dark place for storage.

Processing

Select fruits and vegetables to freeze when they are at their peak of ripeness. Fix any aesthetically challenged produce by cutting out blemishes or bruised areas—just freeze the good stuff. Produce should be cut to the sizes most commonly called for in recipes. For example, you should finely chop onions to use later in sauces, but quarter apples since that is the size most commonly used in pies. Keeping the pieces small means it will take less time to thaw for use, and it reduces the amount of prep work you will need to do when cooking later.

Allow an inch of headspace when packing liquids like soups, stews, and juices into containers with wide lids. If there is a narrow opening to the container, leave $1^1/_2$ inches of headspace. For dry packed foods, like chopped vegetables, berries, and fruit slices, you should be fine with only $^1/_2$ inch of headspace in the container.

Place filled containers and bags into the freezer immediately after packing. Avoid initially stacking unfrozen foods on top of or next to each other. Give them a little elbow room so the cold air can circulate around them, freezing them quicker. After they are frozen you can rearrange them so they are closely packed together.

If you use freezer bags, they should lay flat in the freezer for the initial freeze. Once frozen, it is much easier to stack different bags on top of one another and keeps the freezer nice and organized. If you can't see it, things can get easily lost in there.

Clearly label everything that goes into the freezer and include the date it was processed. I tend to be a little obsessive about how things are ultimately sorted

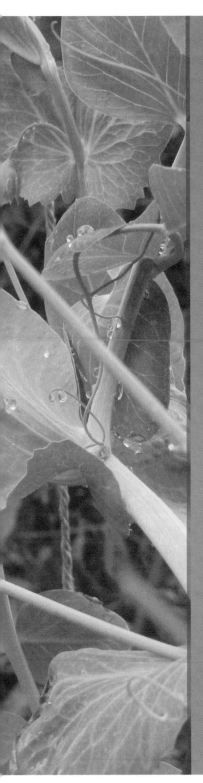

Blanching

Most vegetables need a quick blanch before freezing, which is not nearly as complicated as it sounds. This chart is a guide on what needs to be blanched and for how long. Basically, you throw the vegetables into a pot of boiling water for a few minutes, then into a sink of cold water. Drain, then fill up a freezer bag or container. This will kill off the enzymes that will cause them to deteriorate.

Type	Blanching	Comments
Vegetables		
Artichokes, globe	Yes	8–10 minutes
Artichokes, Jerusalem	N/A	Not recommended for freezing
Asparagus	Yes	3–4 minutes
Beans, bush	Yes	3–4 minutes
Beans, lima	Yes	3–4 minutes
Beans, pole	Yes	3–4 minutes
Beans, for drying	No	Freeze dried beans as is
Beets	N/A	Must be cooked prior to freezing
Broccoli	Yes	3–5 minutes
Brussels sprouts	Yes	4–6 minutes
Cabbage	Yes	3–4 minutes
Carrots	Yes	3–5 minutes
Cauliflower	Yes	3–5 minutes
Celery	Yes	3–4 minutes
Corn	Yes	4–6 minutes
Cucumbers	N/A	Not recommended for freezing
Eggplant	Yes	4–6 minutes
Kale	Yes	2–3 minutes
Kohlrabi	Yes	3–4 minutes
Leeks	No	
Onions	No	
Parsnips	Yes	3–5 minutes
Peas, shelling	Yes	2–3 minutes
Peas, snap	Yes	2–3 minutes
Peppers, hot	Yes	2 minutes
Peppers, sweet	Yes	2 minutes
Potatoes	N/A	Not recommended for freezing
Pumpkin	No	Must be cooked prior to freezing
Radishes	N/A	Not recommended for freezing
Rutabagas	Yes	3–4 minutes
Soybeans	Yes	5 minutes
Spinach	Yes	2–3 minutes
Squash, winter	No	Must be cooked prior to freezing
Squash, summer	N/A	Not recommended for freezing
Sweet potatoes	N/A	Not recommended for freezing
Swiss chard	Yes	2–3 minutes
Tomatoes	No	Must be cooked prior to freezing
Turnips	Yes	2–3 minutes

Type	Blanching
Fruits	
Apples	No
Apricots	No
Blackberries	No
Blueberries	No
Boysenberries	No
Cherries, sweet	No
Cherries, sour	No
Currants	No
Gooseberries	No
Grapes	No
Melon	No
Peaches	No
Pears	No
Persimmons	No
Plums	No
Raspberries	No
Rhubarb	No
Strawberries	No

Frozen snow peas are excellent in stir-fries or tossed salads.

in the freezer. Vegetables go in one section, fruits in another, and meat in yet another spot. I want that door to be open as briefly as possible in the winter when I need to grab something. I also keep a tally of every bag, container, or wrapped package that goes in by posting a list on the fridge. We check things off as they get used, making it easy to see what we have in there without even opening the freezer door.

Fruits and vegetables will stay fresh in the freezer for eight to twelve months, although I have found buried produce in there from over a year ago that has tasted just fine. Poultry generally keeps fresh for six to nine months. Ground meat and fish keeps for three to six months. These are prime freshness times. It took us over a year to eat all the beef we bought from a local farmer, and it tasted just fine when we cooked it up.

Pesto ingredients: basil, pine nuts, Parmesan, and garlic.

Recipes

Presto Pesto

Having a container of homemade pesto in the freezer is like having an instant meal on hand at all times. Pesto can be added to so many dishes to jazz them up with homegrown flavor: simple cooked noodles, cheese ravioli, lasagna, baked chicken, broiled fish, and so on. If you grow your own basil, make several batches of pesto throughout the summer. It will keep your freezer packed and also encourage your basil to continually fill out with more leaves.

- 2 cups fresh basil, packed
- $\frac{1}{3}$ cup olive oil, more if needed
- 3–4 cloves garlic
- $\frac{1}{2}$ cup pine nuts
- $\frac{1}{2}$ cup grated Parmesan cheese
- Salt and pepper to taste

1. Using a food processor or blender, mix basil, oil, and garlic until finely ground.
2. Add in pine nuts and Parmesan cheese and process until desired consistency. Add salt and pepper to taste.
3. Pesto is good left chunky or puréed smooth. Store in an airtight container in the freezer for up to a year. Use a knife to scrape out the amount you need, rather than defrosting the entire container and refreezing. This can change the flavor if done too many times.

Fruit Popsicles

We can pretend this is a recipe you will use for the kids, but let's be honest: Popsicles in the summer have no age restrictions. I made these every week when we lived in Brooklyn with no air conditioner. They come in handy during the peak of a sweltering harvest season.

- 1 cup simple syrup
- 1 cup peaches, sliced
- 1 cup blueberries
- 1 tablespoon lime juice

1. To make the simple syrup, mix $1/2$ cup of water with $1/2$ cup of sugar and heat until boiling. Once the sugar has dissolved, remove from heat and let the mixture cool.
2. In a blender or food processor, combine cooled syrup with peaches and blueberries until smooth. Pour into reusable Popsicle molds, or use paper cups with wooden sticks placed in the middle, and freeze.

CAN IT

A few extra hours in the kitchen during the gardening season will reward you with cupboards stocked to the brim with delicious homemade preserves. You can do small canning batches with fruit gathered from your own backyard or produce purchased at bulk rates from the nearest farm or market. Once you begin the journey into canning your own produce, you will be reluctant to ever pay money for bland store-bought goods again.

Methods

There are two general methods to safely preserve food through canning: a hot water bath or steam-pressure canner. The hot water bath method requires only a pot of boiling water to submerge your preserves into for a given period of time. The steam-pressure canner is a much more costly kitchen item, but this method offers you a wider array of food options to can.

The hot water bath method works only on high-acid foods. The good news is that most of the canned goods you will be interested in preserving fall into this category: jam, jelly, preserves, chutney, pickles, and tomatoes. Minimal equipment is needed as well. Try just using a jerry-rigged stockpot to preserve a couple jars of jam if you are just starting out and are unsure about purchasing all the gear. If you succeed and

From left to right: spicy pickles, halved peaches, honey-vinegar carrots.

Tomato skins peel off easily after being immersed in boiling water for sixty seconds.

want to make more, think about upgrading to some better equipment.

A steam-pressure canner is a bigger financial commitment that opens more doors in food preservation. With a pressure canner, you can put up batches of stew, soup, meat, fish, and low-acid produce like green beans, peas, corn, and carrots, all canned in water. With a hot water bath, these low-acid foods would need to be pickled instead of canned in water.

A steam-pressure canner lets you say good-bye to ever needing to buy canned vegetables. Just buy in bulk from the closest farm during the peak production time or harvest from your own garden, spend a few hours in the kitchen, and stock the cupboards with farm-fresh vegetables.

Basic Supplies

Whichever canning method you decide on, there are a few supplies you need to acquire before diving in. If you want to explore the hot water bath method, you should consider buying a large metal canner, which is essentially a very large stockpot with a wire rack inside. The rack will hold your jars, allowing you to easily drop them in or lift them out of the boiling water. It also ensures the boiling water can evenly circulate on all sides of the jars for even cooking.

Hot water bath canners are not terribly expensive and can commonly be found secondhand. Check estate sales, thrift stores, and online classified ads for deals. They can also be purchased new from department stores, hardware stores, and home improvement centers. Depending on the size, they tend to range from $20 to $30.

You can also use a regular old stockpot for canning a few jars at a time. The pot needs to be large enough so the jars can be covered with at least two inches of water. Also, the jars should not rest on the bottom of the pot, so keep your eyes peeled for a small wire rack that can be placed on the bottom of the pot. This ensures the boiling water can surround the whole jar and heat it evenly and thoroughly.

It took me a few weeks to find something to fit my stockpot, but eventually I found a discarded round wire rack that I think was used for cooling baked goods. It has made a perfect retrofitted canner, and I loan it out to my friends who are dabbling in canning. Eventually many of them are bitten by the homesteading bug and end up buying an actual canner, since you are able to can more jars at a time in it.

If you decide to experiment with the steam-pressure canner, I recommend borrowing one from a friend or relative before investing in one yourself, especially if you are new to canning. They are expensive, ranging from $75 to well over $100, so you want to be sure you will use it often. Perhaps you have a friend who shares your interest in canning and you can go in on one together, taking turns using it.

When using a pressure canner, check the gauge annually to make sure everything is in working order. The instruction manual will give you directions on doing this for your machine. If you buy a pressure canner secondhand and the manual has been lost, call your local extension office and they can help you find instructions to check the gauge.

Canners come in a few different sizes, so consider where you can store it and how often you plan to can. If you have seasonal storage space for the canner and have plans to stock up on huge batches

of tomatoes to feed a family of four, get the largest size available—it will save you time in the long run. However, if you are a single person or a couple and have a kitchen the size of a closet, consider the smaller sizes for canning in small batches throughout the season.

After you get your hands on a canner, you will need to stock up on canning jars and lids. These items are easily found at grocery stores, hardware stores, and home improvement centers. Not every glass jar is appropriate for canning—some are too

Marinara sauce makes meal prep easy all winter. Use it for spaghetti, lasagna, or as pizza sauce.

thin and break—so don't try to reuse glass jars from grocery items. Comb garage sales and estate sales or look for good sales in late summer and fall. Good canning jars can be reused from one season to the next, so consider it a small investment in your canning future.

Two-piece caps consist of a metal ring and a metal flat cap. The caps cannot be reused, as their sealing agent wears out. The metal rings, however, can be used over and over again, assuming they stay clean and rust free. Keep your overall costs low by saving jars and rings from one season to the next. Buy the metal caps in larger packages for additional savings and to ensure you are always prepared for a last-minute midnight batch of jam.

Take my advice and get your canning supplies together before you actually decide to cook up some preserves. Of course this sounds straightforward, and of course I have failed to do this before. Poor Jay had to run to three grocery stores one September evening because the first two were sold out of jars and lids. Canning gets more popular every year, and sometimes places run out. Shop around for deals, but shop in advance of bringing home thirty pounds of tomatoes.

Generally you will find Ball and Kerr are the largest players when it comes to canning jars and lids, and they can look pretty basic. They are starting to get the hint that canning can also be hip, and Ball recently came out with a line of vintage-inspired canning jars. Smaller companies like Leifheit offer fancier jars that are becoming more widely available.

Check online retailers to see what is available. Just make sure whatever jars and lids you get are specifically for canning so you know they will seal properly.

Making-Life-Easier Supplies

Regardless of the canning method you use, there are a few smaller, inexpensive items that are recommended to help prevent hot splatters and burns during canning. I held off on buying these for years because I am thrifty (that is, cheap). In hindsight, I regret not buying these inexpensive supplies sooner. I would have had far fewer burns and tomato-stained clothes.

I highly recommend a jar lifter, which is basically a set of tongs with rounded rubber grabbers. It fits snuggly with a firm grip around the circular tops of your jars, which prevents them from slipping into the boiling water, splashing you and everything around you.

Next, consider buying a wide-mouthed funnel. I tried for a couple years to use a regular funnel, and pretty much everything gets clogged in the narrow spout—sticky berry preserves, thick marinara sauce, etc. The top rims of the glass jars need to be absolutely clean for proper sealing with the lids. Most of my canning failures can be attributed to the jar rim not being fully wiped off. A wide-mouthed funnel helps you fill the jars faster without leaving anything on the rims.

An additional item that might be nice to have around is a large thermometer. This will take the guessing-game element out of trying to determine if jelly has been heated up enough to set. There are other tests you can do to determine when things have been cooked enough to can, but this will make things a bit easier.

As canning becomes more and more popular, canning kits are popping up that combine all of these recommended smaller tools into one package. The cost is relatively low, like $15, and they make the canning experience all that much more pleasant.

It is a wonderful thing to take a few hours throughout the growing season to put away small batches of homemade, organic goodies. But pace yourself so you don't burn out and, if you can afford the cost and space, add a few items to make your life easier.

What to Can

High-acid foods can be safely canned using the hot water bath method. This includes all fruits and tomatoes. To ensure the acidity level is high enough, lemon juice or pectin is often added during the canning process, which does not have a strong effect on the overall flavor.

Other vegetables and all meats/fish need to be canned with a pressure canner because they require a temperature higher than that of boiling water in order to be properly preserved. That said, some vegetables make good candidates for pickling, which can be done with a water bath. Vinegar is added to raise the overall acidity level of these low-acid foods.

Homemade canned goods make thoughtful gifts.

The chart in this chapter can guide you in how to preserve your harvest. Mix and match fruits to make new variations of jams and preserves. Experiment by using preserves as a cupcake filling. The recipes out there in the culinary world are endlessly inspiring.

Tips

Canning involves cooking, which can heat up a kitchen pretty quickly. Spring and fall temperatures may be cool enough to allow for comfortable canning during the day, but plan on evening canning sessions in the hot summer months. Keep an eye on the forecast when you are planning to can, and set your schedule accordingly.

Let a slow cooker help you out with things like ketchup, marinara sauce, or fruit butters. These require longer cooking times to develop a thick end product. They also require constant stirring so the mixture does not burn, and it gets mighty tiresome standing over a pot stirring constantly for an hour. A slow cooker ensures the mixture does not burn, and constant babysitting is not required. Set the cooker on low and leave the lid ajar slightly so some moisture can escape. You can cook things down overnight and process them in jars the next morning, freeing up the rest of your day.

Always wear long sleeves when you are canning, to avoid burns. Hot preserves bubble, and boiling water can splatter, often when you are inches away stirring them. You should also avoid wearing shorts or skirts, and never wear open-toed shoes. It really stinks when you are

carrying a pot of boiling jam to the table to begin filling jars only to have the slippery sucker fall out of your hands and onto the floor. That would be approxi-

Wine and snacks make canning more enjoyable.

mately a million times worse if said spill landed all over your lovely bare toes.

I make a point to have finger food handy whenever I can. It just doesn't seem fair to cook something that fills the whole house with an amazing aroma and not be simultaneously eating something delicious. Often canning turns into a longer affair than I planned, and it takes much longer if you need to stop for lunch. Things like chips and salsa, pita and hummus, cookies, crackers, and cheese are all fun to munch on, and they keep your energy level high.

Time tends to fly by much faster in the kitchen when I am rocking out to some good tunes. I set up a long, long playlist before I turn on any stove. A playlist, rather than individual CDs or records, disguises the time lapse. When you have had to change a CD or record out three times, you are extremely aware that you have spent three hours canning. If you have a three-hour playlist, you play a mental trick on yourself by not repeating anything you have heard, which makes you less aware of how much time has gone by.

A very important tip on canning: invite over a friend or two. Splitting the cost on a huge batch of produce and canning it together makes the experience way more fun. It is just as easy to catch up with friends while canning chutney as it is to sit around over a glass of wine. And hey, why be exclusionary? Open some wine and make chutney together at the same time.

Don't Poison Yourself: Avoiding Botulism

The process of canning destroys most of the microorganisms on food that can develop into harmful bacteria, yeasts, and molds. It also creates a strong vacuum that prevents new air, with microorganisms along for the ride, from entering into the jars and resulting in spoilage.

The largest fear associated with canning is botulism, a deadly version of food poisoning that results from eating food contaminated with the bacterium *Clostridium botulinum*. The bacteria are odorless, flavorless, and invisible. You can see where all of the intense warnings come from.

Don't be scared by canning books that beat you over the head with horror stories of poisoning yourself and loved ones with botulism. Canning can be lovely and simple, but you need to play by the rules for safe food storage. You don't need to be a rocket scientist—just be smart about the process.

First, start with good canning jars that have been thoroughly cleaned with warm soapy water. After washing them, I place mine in the clean water bath canner while I wait for the water to boil, which acts as a second round of sterilizing before the jars are filled. I remove them from the canner, fill with my hot prepared foods, adjust the two-piece caps, then put them right back in the canner for the recommended cooking time. Don't cut corners.

Second, check the seals on your canned goods before putting them away in the cupboard and again before opening them to eat. The lids should be suctioned down and should pop when you open them for use. If you don't hear the lids pop down within twenty-four hours of canning, double-check the seal by pressing the tops down to see if they are suctioned. Heat the contents back up and recan with new lids if they have not suctioned down.

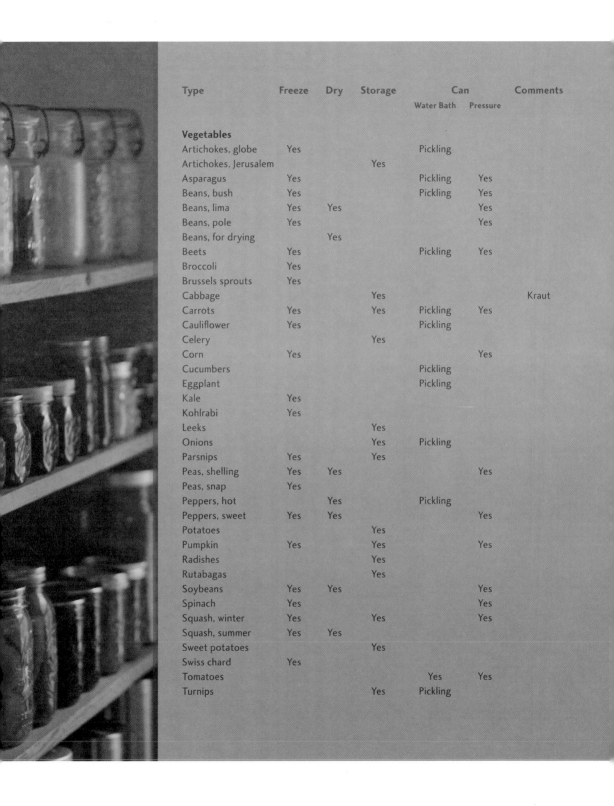

Type	Freeze	Dry	Storage	Can Water Bath	Can Pressure	Comments
Vegetables						
Artichokes, globe	Yes			Pickling		
Artichokes, Jerusalem			Yes			
Asparagus	Yes			Pickling	Yes	
Beans, bush	Yes			Pickling	Yes	
Beans, lima	Yes	Yes			Yes	
Beans, pole	Yes				Yes	
Beans, for drying		Yes				
Beets	Yes			Pickling	Yes	
Broccoli	Yes					
Brussels sprouts	Yes					
Cabbage			Yes			Kraut
Carrots	Yes		Yes	Pickling	Yes	
Cauliflower	Yes			Pickling		
Celery			Yes			
Corn	Yes				Yes	
Cucumbers				Pickling		
Eggplant				Pickling		
Kale	Yes					
Kohlrabi	Yes					
Leeks			Yes			
Onions			Yes	Pickling		
Parsnips	Yes		Yes			
Peas, shelling	Yes	Yes			Yes	
Peas, snap	Yes					
Peppers, hot		Yes		Pickling		
Peppers, sweet	Yes	Yes			Yes	
Potatoes			Yes			
Pumpkin	Yes		Yes		Yes	
Radishes			Yes			
Rutabagas			Yes			
Soybeans	Yes	Yes			Yes	
Spinach	Yes				Yes	
Squash, winter	Yes		Yes		Yes	
Squash, summer	Yes	Yes				
Sweet potatoes			Yes			
Swiss chard	Yes					
Tomatoes				Yes	Yes	
Turnips			Yes	Pickling		

Type	Freeze	Dry	Storage	Can	
				Water Bath	Pressure
Fruits					
Apples	Yes	Yes	Yes	Yes	Yes
Apricots		Yes		Yes	Yes
Blackberries	Yes			Yes	Yes
Blueberries	Yes	Yes		Yes	Yes
Boysenberries	Yes	Yes		Yes	Yes
Cherries, sweet	Yes	Yes		Yes	Yes
Cherries, sour	Yes			Yes	Yes
Currants	Yes	Yes		Yes	Yes
Gooseberries	Yes	Yes		Yes	Yes
Grapes		Yes		Yes	Yes
Melons	Yes		Yes		
Peaches	Yes	Yes		Yes	Yes
Pears		Yes	Yes	Yes	Yes
Persimmons	Yes				Yes
Plums	Yes	Yes		Yes	Yes
Raspberries	Yes			Yes	Yes
Rhubarb				Yes	Yes
Strawberries	Yes	Yes		Yes	Yes

Acidity levels tend to decline as fruits and vegetables become overripe. You want to use fresh produce that has just reached its prime or produce that is even slightly underripe. Just like you would do with any food preservation method, cut out any bruises or blemishes and discard them. These are areas where molds and bacteria will first begin to develop.

Although I do not technically recommend this for others, there have been a few occasions where I have followed *most* but not *all* of the rules on a recipe. I may have decided to tweak the seasonings slightly, or maybe I forgot to add a teaspoon of lemon juice to my canned tomatoes. The tomatoes were good quality and the lemon juice is typically a peace-of-mind ingredient that ensures a high acidity level.

In these cases I usually call my grandma Egger to ask for her advice. Often my questions are met with this type of response: "Oh, I've been canning tomatoes for years and I never add lemon juice" or "I usually just make up the herb mix as I go when I can marinara sauce." That usually makes me feel like whatever little mistake I made was, in most cases, not bad enough to warrant throwing out the batch.

Throw a Canning Party

Canning can be a lot more enjoyable with company there to pitch in and share the harvest, so invite some friends over for a canning party. Especially if you live in a one- or two-person household, it can be difficult to get bulk deals on produce for the amount of canned goods you will use in a year or grow enough tomatoes to make large batches of marinara sauce. With friends there to split the cost and the canned goods, you can pool your money to get deals on produce or pool your produce to make larger batches of food together.

You can either acquire all of the canning jars and lids prior to the party and divide up the cost or ask people to bring their own. It typically works best for one person to buy all of the produce and smaller ingredients, so have someone round up the goods before the party and everyone can settle up when they arrive for the soirée.

In preparation for the party, have a nice, long song mix ready to rock. Plan for a three-hour mix of your favorite songs to keep things moving—nothing too low key. Ask everyone to bring a dish you can eat with your hands, like stuffed mushrooms, phyllo dough pastries, and the like. Wine and beer are usually warmly welcomed too, helping with the flow of the day.

Marinara sauce can be a good choice for a canning party because it is so versatile to use and easy to plan a party theme around. I like to host a movie and marinara canning party so we can play off the Italian-themed sauce while giving it ample time to simmer down on the stove.

Canning with friends is entertaining and productive.

Always wear long sleeves when canning to prevent burns. Gently drop tomatoes in hot water to loosen their skins.

In the past we have chosen mobster movies like *Heat*, foreign films like *La Strada*, and classic love stories like *Moonstruck* to keep us entertained. See what your friends are in the mood for—bloodlust or simply just lust—and party plan accordingly.

Pause the movie halfway through to begin processing the jars. As the jars simmer in the hot water bath, you can finish the last half of the movie. When the film is over, it's time for everyone to go home with piping hot jars of delicious marinara.

Keep It Fun

I cannot stress enough what a big difference food on hand, something to listen to, and company can make to the whole canning experience. You need to keep your energy up to get through the process. Catching up with a friend is a great way to spend time together and also walk away with some delicious canned goods. If you need to can alone, think about listening to your favorite podcast or using a goofy headset to talk on the phone with family while you stir preserves.

I am reminded of the taste of summer every time I reach into my cupboards in the winter and pop open a jar of rich berry preserves or delicious chutney. It makes those extra hours I spent canning completely worth it.

Recipes

Saucy Marinara

- 30 pounds sauce tomatoes
- 4 onions, chopped
- 4 cloves garlic, minced
- 2 cups dried basil
- 1 cup honey
- 2 bay leaves
- 3 tablespoons each dried oregano, thyme, parsley
- 3 tablespoons salt
- 2 teaspoons pepper
- 1 teaspoon each cinnamon, nutmeg
- 2 teaspoons vanilla extract
- 7 teaspoons lemon juice

1. Wash and sterilize seven quart jars or fourteen pint jars.
2. Bring a pot of water to a boil. Working in batches, drop tomatoes into boiling water for thirty seconds. Plunge tomatoes into ice-cold water. Peel skins off and cut out core. Purée tomatoes in a blender.
3. In a large stockpot, simmer onions and garlic with a little tomato purée until softened. Add all other ingredients except lemon juice and bring to a simmer, stirring occasionally, for one hour on low heat, or until desired thickness is achieved. Remove bay leaves.
4. Fill canner with water and bring to a boil. Add lemon juice to sauce. Working in batches, ladle sauce into jars, leaving about one inch of headspace. Wipe rim of jars with a damp cloth to ensure a clean surface. Immediately adjust two-piece caps. Submerge in canner of boiling water for forty-five minutes. Remove and cool.

Marinara sauce in smaller containers works well for one- to two-person servings.

Forest Berry Preserves

- 4 cups berries: any mixture of blackberries, strawberries, raspberries, marionberries, blueberries, huckleberries
- 2 cups sugar
- Zest from 1 lemon

1. Wash and sterilize four half-pint jars.
2. In a large stockpot, mix berries with sugar and let sit for fifteen minutes.
3. Add lemon zest and, over moderate heat, bring berry mixture to a boil. Simmer the mixture, stirring often to prevent sticking to the bottom, until it has reduced to a thick consistency. If you scoop it onto a spoon, it should stay loosely mounded. In other words, it should not flow off in a liquid stream but should be a bit chunky.
4. Bring the canner to a boil. Ladle the preserves into the jars, leaving a half inch of headspace. Wipe the glass rims. Adjust two-piece caps. Boil the filled jars for ten minutes. Let cool.

Preserves are ready when they mound on a spoon and hold their shape.

Asian Pear Chutney

- 6 pounds Asian pears, peeled, cored, and roughly chopped
- 2 cups brown sugar
- $\frac{1}{2}$ cup dried golden raisins
- $\frac{1}{2}$ cup dried cranberries
- 2 onions, chopped
- $\frac{1}{4}$ cup mustard seed
- 3 tablespoons ginger
- 2 teaspoons salt
- 2 cloves garlic, minced
- 1 hot pepper, minced
- 2 cups apple cider vinegar
- 3 cups white vinegar

1. Wash and sterilize seven pint jars.
2. Combine all of the ingredients in a large stockpot over medium-high heat and bring to a boil. Simmer the mixture, stirring occasionally, until it has reduced to $\frac{1}{4}$ of its original volume. Stir more toward the end to prevent sticking.
3. Bring a canner of water to a boil. Ladle the hot mixture into jars, leaving a half inch of headspace. Wipe the rims clean with a damp cloth and adjust two-piece caps. Submerge in boiling water for fifteen minutes. Cool.

Great Aunt Dot's Fig Preserves

Marrying Jay meant that I gained a whole new rich family history. This recipe comes from his family down South and has become a staple in our household as well. It's an easy recipe, figs grow all over the country, and it looks great in the jar.

- 1 quart freshly picked figs
- 1 pint sugar
- 1 lemon, cut into thin slices
- water

1. Wash and sterilize four half-pint jars.
2. Mix all of the ingredients in a Dutch oven and fill with enough water to cover. Boil the mixture for two hours, until the figs begin to look transparent.
3. Bring a canner of water to a boil. Ladle the hot mixture into jars, leaving a half inch of headspace. Wipe the rims clean with a damp cloth and adjust two-piece caps. Submerge in boiling water for fifteen minutes. Cool.

Dry It

Drying foods is a simple and space-saving way to preserve the harvest. Dried berries and fruit are delicious, healthy snacks to get you through the winter months. Dried vegetables add a punch of flavor when cooked into stews, soups, and casseroles. Although not as sexy as a jar of jam, dried foods tend to retain more of their nutritional content than canned.

As a preservation method, the drying process removes 80 to 90 percent of the moisture in food. This creates an uninhabitable environment for food spoilers like bacteria, yeast, and molds. When done properly, dried foods can last anywhere from six months to a couple years. Roughly four pounds of fresh produce will dry down to about one pound—lightweight and taking up little space in the cupboard. If you live in a tiny apartment or condo, drying the harvest may be an excellent option with your digs in mind.

The key to properly dried foods is air circulation and warm temperatures. Air needs to reach under, over, and around the sides of the foods you are drying. The ideal drying process does several things: air circulates evenly, hot temperatures are slow and steady for evaporation, and food is protected from insects and pollutants. When drying food, maintaining the perfect temperature is often the trickiest aspect to control.

If the temperature is too low, it will take forever to dry the food or it may not dry out at all. You also run the risk of encouraging bacteria to multiply, which is bad, bad news. The drying temperature needs to stay above 95 degrees Fahrenheit to prevent this from happening.

If the temperature is too high, you will end up cooking the food instead of drying it. The outside cooks and creates a hard outer shell, trapping moisture inside the food, which is called case hardening. The trapped moisture will eventually cause spoilage. The hot temperature may have also killed off valuable nutrients and vitamins. You will want to keep the temperature below 140 degrees Fahrenheit to avoid cooking your beloved produce.

Methods

Food is typically dehydrated using one of the following methods: dry air and hot sun, the oven, or a food dehydrator. Of these methods, the food dehydrator offers the most control over the drying process in terms of air circulation, protection from unwanted particles and bugs, and keeping a steady, proper temperature throughout the process.

Using the sun to dry food is simple and rather straightforward. You will need about three days of hot, sunny weather with low humidity. In some climates, this can be most of the days of the year. In others, you may need to wait until late August to have a hot enough, dry enough few days. It is not recommended to use this method if you live in an area of high pollution, like Manhattan, where city pollutants in the air will settle on your otherwise delicious and nutritious food.

Determine in advance where the best place will be to dry your food by hanging a thermometer outside in different locations. Ideally you want a place that will have a temperature range of 95 to 130 degrees Fahrenheit. Look for little microclimates, like near a dark exterior wall or in an unvegetated corner of the yard.

Food should be set out on racks to dry in the morning, when all dew has evaporated. Racks can be made from a variety of material including thin wood, nylon, or cheesecloth, but metal should be avoided as it can have unwanted reactions with food. The racks, raised above the ground, allow air to circulate over and under the cut pieces. To protect the food from bugs and dust, cover it loosely with cheesecloth. Air can still penetrate underneath while there is a barrier to tiny critters and things floating through the air. Turn the food pieces often throughout the day to encourage even drying.

Depending on how much the temperature drops at night, you can cover the drying racks with a towel to absorb any nighttime moisture. Or simply bring the trays inside and set up again in the morning if it gets too cool or damp at night.

Some people choose to up the ante on outdoor drying by building a simple homemade solar dehydrator. The constructed frame should be fairly airtight, but have a few vent holes drilled in for continual air circulation. Ideally the vents will close at night, to prevent losing too much heat. A thermometer hanging inside helps to monitor the temperature throughout the drying process. Some folks get even fancier and include a fan inside to help move air around.

Solar dryers can be as complex or

Thinly sliced fruit dries more quickly.

simple as you have the motivation for. On the simple end of the spectrum, use old windows to surround the drying trays. This increases the intensity of both the sunlight and heat while protecting the food from bugs. Using foil on the walls will direct additional sunlight onto the trays. Use your creativity to put together something that works for you with salvaged or found materials. It doesn't need to be fancy to be useful.

Ovens set on low bake temperatures can also be used for drying foods, although they suck up lots of electricity. Hang a thermometer inside the oven, as the temperature can easily get too hot and end up cooking your food to pieces. The temperature should never exceed 140 degrees Fahrenheit. The warm setting can help you hover in this range.

Place food directly on the racks and rotate the racks in the oven often for even drying. Begin with the pieces cut-side up, so they dry and harden before you flip them over to dry the other side. Keep a close eye on them, as it can take anywhere from four to twelve hours for the process to be complete.

The most foolproof method of drying food is using a commercially made food dehydrator. Simple models can be found on the cheap at estate sales, garage sales, thrift stores, and through online classifieds. Only consider models that have a thermostat, which most models include.

Food dehydrators can be a little noisy, and they do take up some room. They are only needed during one time of the year, so perhaps you can find room on a shelf in the closet, under the bed, or inside a footstool to house your dehydrator in the off-season. My handy grandfather helped me make a bench whose seats can lift up for storage. This has become my favorite storage space for the dehydrator.

As with other drying methods, rotate the trays throughout the process for even cooking and flip the food pieces periodically. Line the trays with cheesecloth if the openings are too big and food pieces can potentially fall through. Dehydrators with built-in fans are extra helpful for even drying.

Process

Start with good-quality produce for drying. Cut out any bad spots, overripened areas, or bruises. For everything other than herbs, wash thoroughly. Cut food pieces relatively evenly for a uniform drying time. Then determine if the produce needs to be blanched prior to drying.

Blanching is sometimes recommended for low-acid foods—often vegetables and not as often for fruits. It destroys the enzymes in low-acid foods that can deteriorate the flavor over time. It also helps to preserve the color. Blanching also softens the tissue of the food, allowing moisture to escape easier.

Blanching should be done after you are done cutting everything up. Check the chart on pages 154–55 for a guide to recommended blanching times. You can either steam the cut pieces for the recommended time or throw them into a pot of boiling water. Pat the pieces dry to get rid of excess moisture before laying them out on drying racks.

Herbs do not need to be rinsed if they are relatively clean, as washing can remove flavorful oils. Be gentle with them—crushed leaves release flavor oils. Crush them only before use in cooking. Herbs can easily be dried by hanging them upside down in a place away from moisture, as they require lower temperatures than vegetables and fruits.

The ideal drying temperature for herbs is roughly 100 degrees Fahrenheit. Fruits and vegetables should be dried somewhere around 120 to 130 degrees. Meats and fish should be dried at higher temperatures, around 145 degrees. Use a dehydrator for fish and meat, and follow the manufacturer's instructions carefully.

Drying is complete when the food is leathery but still pliable. The exceptions to this are beans, peas, and corn, which should all be hard when done. Remove a piece and let it cool when you think a batch is done. Once cooled, check the texture to determine if it is ready for storage. Dried foods can sometimes harden further once cooled. Remove individual pieces as they dry, rather than removing them all at once.

Store your dried goodies separately in airtight ceramic, glass, or plastic containers. Wood should be avoided because it breathes and can allow in moisture. Metal should also be avoided because it can leave a metallic taste on the food, unless you line the container with a plastic or paper bag.

This is your opportunity to make dried goods look more attractive, so shop around for pretty containers. I buy cases of vintage glass jars from estate sales.

They are no longer recommended for canning, but they work well for holding dried goods. Arranged on a shelf together, they give me a sense that I have a well-stocked homestead.

Give the stored goods a good turn after about a week to make sure the moisture level is even in the container. You can always dry it a little more if it seems too moist. Drying is nice and forgiving in that way. A dark, cool but not cold place is best for storage—like your kitchen cupboards. How convenient!

Most fruits will keep for up to six months or more. Dried vegetables' life span varies anywhere from two to six months. Try a nibble first to make sure it still tastes great. I will openly admit to eating dried goods well over six months that tasted just fine.

Using Dried Foods

Most dried fruits can be enjoyed without reconstituting, but vegetables often need to be plumped back up before use in cooking. Pour boiling water over dried food pieces and cover until tender to reconstitute. Steaming may work better for tender greens.

The best way to cook with dried vegetables is to add them into soups, stews, and casseroles. They can be added in already dried; just add more liquid to the dish than the recipe calls for. Typically one cup of liquid to one cup of dried vegetables is a good measure. The vegetables will soak up delicious broths and add a wonderful flavor in return. One cup of dried vegetables equals about two to four cups fresh.

Recipes

Aunt Emily's Italian Seasoning

My aunt Emily is a fabulous cook and created the following herb blend. The versatile mix is excellent in pastas, as a chicken seasoning, baked into dinner breads, or mixed into butter that gets spread over vegetables. It's no replacement for her home-cooked meals, but it is certainly a welcomed friend in the spice rack.

- $^1/_2$ tablespoon rosemary
- 2 tablespoons parsley
- $^1/_2$ tablespoon sage
- $^1/_2$ tablespoon oregano
- 2 tablespoons basil
- 1 tablespoon thyme

1. Mix all ingredients until well distributed.
2. Store in a clean glass spice jar in a cool, dark place. Crush before use to release optimum flavor.

Herb Bouquets

You can use any combination you like, but I prefer to arrange herb bouquets with the fewest number of the largest herbs and increase the sprig number as the herbs become finer.

- 1 sprig rosemary
- 2 sprigs oregano
- 3 sprigs sage
- 4 sprigs thyme

1. Using a piece of gardener's twine, wrap the herbs together tightly and hang upside down to dry for two or three days.
2. Give to friends at housewarming or dinner parties for use in vegetable stocks, or for darling decorations.

Herb Butter

- 2 tablespoons dried herbs
- 1 cup butter, softened

1. Mix all ingredients until well combined.
2. Refrigerate for six hours for flavors to mingle.
3. Serve with bread, over steamed vegetables, or use as a base for sautés.

Homegrown Trail Mix

This is an excellent snack for both kids and adults that can be tailored to suit your own backyard harvest. Kids will especially enjoy mixing their own special snack blend!

- 2 cups oats
- 1 cup almonds
- 1 cup hazelnuts
- $1/2$ cup pumpkin seeds
- $1/2$ cup sunflower seeds
- $1/2$ cup honey
- $1/4$ cup butter, melted
- $1/2$ cup dried raisins
- $1/2$ cup dried cherries
- 1 cup dried apricots, chopped

1. Preheat oven to 300 degrees Fahrenheit.
2. Mix oats, nuts, seeds, honey, and butter together and bake in the oven for thirty minutes, turning every ten minutes, until well toasted. Remove from oven and cool.
3. Once cool, toss with the dried fruit and store in an airtight container. The mixture should stay fresh for about a week.

Sun-Dried Tomato Dip

This dip makes a great appetizer paired with thick country bread or crackers.

- $^1/_2$ cup sun-dried tomatoes
- 2 cups boiling water
- 2 cups plain yogurt
- 1 garlic clove, minced
- 2 tablespoons fresh basil, chopped
- Salt and pepper to taste

1. Cover the tomatoes completely with boiling water, cover, and let stand for thirty minutes. When they have plumped up, drain and reserve soaking liquid.
2. Use a food processor or blender to finely mince tomatoes. Combine with yogurt, garlic, and basil. Add about $^1/_4$ cup of the reserved soaking liquid. Add salt and pepper to taste.
3. Refrigerate overnight to allow the flavors to develop fully, the garlic to mellow out a bit, and the tomatoes to absorb more moisture, making the dip a little thicker.

Tom's Summer Squash Crackers

My farming friend Tom makes these squash rounds in his solar dehydrator as a substitute for crackers with dip or cheese.

- Zucchini or yellow summer squash
- Salt and pepper to taste

1. Thinly slice summer squash and arrange on dehydrator.
2. Lightly sprinkle with salt and pepper to taste.
3. Dry until leathery but still pliable.

Dried tomatoes are great in dips, casseroles, and soups.

These basic natural ingredients can be found at most supermarkets.

HOUSEHOLD CLEANERS

Keeping our homesteads clean and tidy may be a much simpler process than we ever knew. With a little time and creativity, you can easily make your own nontoxic household cleaners. This will almost always be a cost-saving option, and it can be really tempting to experiment with different scents and recipes to find the best fit. You may be surprised to learn that the most common ingredients are ones you already own.

In addition to saving money, making your own household cleaners is a way to ensure you know exactly what ingredients are inside. (Store-bought "green cleaners" can still have ingredients we should avoid.) New studies and articles substantiate growing concerns over the health risks of using toxic chemical household cleaners, so we need to go back to basics. That totally sterile home environment we were once trying to achieve may have actually been hurting us all these years by weakening our immune systems and exposing us to some pretty scary substances. Homemade green cleaners are a better choice for our health and also for our feathered and finned friends in the larger ecosystem.

Supplies

To get started on your green homestead, here is a list of supplies you should have on hand for do-it-yourself cleaners:

Baking soda
Mineral water
Distilled white vinegar
Hydrogen peroxide
Olive oil
Natural vegetable-based liquid soap
   (such as Dr. Bronner's)
Washing soda
Borax
Essential oils

Vinegar is a very versatile cleaner that is both economical and biodegradable.

A couple of these ingredients you may not be familiar with: borax and washing soda. Borax is the common name for sodium borate, a naturally occurring substance. It is a very versatile cleaning ingredient that comes in powder form.

Borax acts as a deodorizer, nonabrasive scouring powder, all-purpose cleaner, mold inhibitor, rust and stain remover.

Washing soda is the common name for sodium carbonate, a substance similar to baking soda that has been processed differently. It is a natural, powerful cleaning ingredient, and you should take care to wear gloves when using it. Washing soda does an excellent job of removing grease stains, oil spots, and wax, and it acts as a deodorizer.

Essential oils should be organic and cold pressed to ensure you are using the highest quality with maximum potency. Some people may have an undesirable sensitivity to certain oils because of their intensity. Pay attention to your body's reaction to the scent of various oils and experiment to find the best ones for you and your family.

You will find that many of the home-made green cleaners in this chapter can be used for multiple purposes. You are not only doing something better for the environment and saving money by making them on your own, but you are also reducing the clutter in your house with unnecessary additional cleaning products.

Simplify

In addition to using green household cleaners, simplifying the products you use in the home can be a healthier option. First, say good-bye to traditional air fresheners. They use chemicals to cover up odors, and they have been implicated in cancer and neurological damage, in addition to having other harmful effects.

Use baking soda instead to naturally neutralize odors by sprinkling a bit around areas that need help. To refresh an entire room, boil a small pot of herbs in water and leave them in the desired space for an hour.

Whenever the weather allows, open the windows to let in clean, fresh air. Even in urban settings, the air outside can often be cleaner than that indoors. Ventilating the house is an opportunity to move out stagnant air filled with germs and let in fresh air. Opening windows at both ends of the house will promote cross-ventilation, moving old air out and new air in. Gotta love that cross-ventilation!

Houseplants not only make indoor spaces more beautiful and welcoming, they act as air purifiers. These natural air filters remove airborne pollutants and release fresh oxygen in return. Be careful not to overwater indoor plants, which promotes mold to form. A few ferns or fig trees here and there can be a welcome improvement for a healthier indoor space.

GREEN BEAUTY

As our modern homesteads become healthier and more productive, it's time we give our beauty regimen a green makeover too. Making your own beauty products is easy and allows you to customize the recipes over time to suit your individual needs. It saves both time and money when you assemble them yourself, relying less on store-bought products.

What goes on our skin, face, and hair eventually makes its way down the drain and into the larger ecosystem. We can still pamper ourselves, but a homemade beauty regimen ensures the ingredients in these products are safe for our bodies and the environment. Homegrown ingredients give you even more control over quality, so look for ingredients from your own garden space, like herbs from the windowsill or beeswax from your backyard hive.

When it comes to beauty, simpler is better. Reducing the number of products we use and how often we use them can lead to less clutter and less time and money spent. For example, one of the best ways to get glossy locks is to not wash our hair every single day. Hair produces oils that give it a shimmery, silky appearance. It responds to being washed and dried out by desperately trying to produce a glut of oil. If we get into the habit of washing our hair every few days, our hair will respond by not producing as many oils.

There are tons of homemade recipes out there to experiment with, and it may take a few tests to find the right ones for you. To begin the process, here are a number of simple homemade recipes you can build from.

Buyer's Guide

Space or time might limit your ability to make your own green household cleaners from scratch. Lucky for you, though, consumer demand is increasing for all-natural products, and companies are responding with eco-friendly alternatives. Be a smart consumer by doing some research before you buy off the shelf. The resources in the reference section at the back of this book will help start your navigation through the cleaner aisle.

To guide you in your quest for green options from the store shelf, only consider products that meet the following guidelines:
- Full disclosure of all product ingredients
- Include only natural and plant-derived ingredients, nothing petroleum based
- Not antibacterial—it kills the good guys too, which is overkill
- Time frame listed for biodegrading as *fast*, *quickly*, or *readily*
- All packaging is recyclable
- No animal testing

Avoid products that include these partial names to describe synthetic ingredients:
- Beginning with *chlor*—chlorinated chemical
- Ending in *ene*—petroleum based
- Ending in *glycol*—petroleum based
- Ending in *phenol*—toxic coal derivative

Do not purchase products that include the following warning signs:
- Flammable—often means it includes hazardous solvents
- Air quality/inhalation warning
- Skin irritation warning
- Warning, danger, or poison label

The Environmental Working Group lists the following ingredients as ones to avoid:
- 2-butoxyethanol (or ethylene glycol monobutyl ether) and other glycol ethers
- Alkylphenol ethoxylates (some common ones are: nonyl- and octylphenol ethoxylates, or non- and octoxynols)
- Dye (companies often hide chemical information behind this word; when it's unknown, it's safer to skip it)
- Ethanolamines (common ones to look out for are mono-, di-, and tri-ethanolamine)
- Fragrance
- Pine or citrus oil (on smoggy or high ozone days, compounds in the oils can react with ozone in the air to form the carcinogenic chemical formaldehyde)
- Quaternary ammonium compounds (look out for alkyl dimethyl benzyl ammonium chloride [ADBAC], benzalkonium chloride, and didecyl dimethyl benzyl ammonium chloride)

Recipes

Lemon All-Purpose Spray

- 1 tablespoon washing soda
- 1 tablespoon borax
- 2 teaspoons vegetable-based liquid soap
- 2 cups hot water
- 3–4 drops lemon essential oil

1. Pour all ingredients into a spray bottle and shake well until fully combined.
2. Spray and wipe down countertops and other surfaces with a reusable rag until dry.

Pine Window Cleaner

- 2 cups water
- 1 cup distilled white vinegar
- 1–2 drops pine essential oil

1. Pour all ingredients into a spray bottle and shake well until fully combined.
2. Use a rag or newspaper to wipe windows after spraying. Once finished, use a clean, soft cloth to wipe away any remaining streaks.
3. The same mixture can be poured into the toilet to clean the bowl.

Tub and Tile Cleaner

- Baking soda
- Water
- 1–2 drops lemon essential oil

1. Dust baking soda on the sink, tub, or tile surface for cleaning.
2. Using a spray bottle containing a mixture of water and the drops of essential oil, mist the area and begin scrubbing with a brush. A thin paste will form as you work the surface, removing grime and built-up residue.

Laundry Soap

- ½ bar Fels-Naptha natural soap (found at grocery stores in the laundry aisle), grated
- ½ cup borax
- ½ cup washing soda
- 1½ gallons water

1. Melt grated soap in a large saucepan with half a gallon of water. Add washing soda and borax, stirring to combine.
2. In a two-gallon bucket, mix soap mixture with another gallon of water and allow to rest overnight.
3. Use ½ cup of the laundry soap per load.

Mix well to prevent lumps. One batch will last for a dozen loads.

Lavender Hand Salve

This recipe uses beeswax, a by-product from the honey-making process available at natural grocery stores or from your own hive. This salve makes an excellent gift and eases chapped skin.

- $^1/_2$ cup dried lavender flowers
- 1 cup olive oil
- 2 tablespoons beeswax
- 1–2 drops essential oil (optional)

1. Using a double boiler, place herbs and oil in top pan and cover with a lid. Simmer mixture for a couple hours, checking occasionally to make sure the oil does not fry the lavender. Strain the herbs out and discard.
2. Return oil back to top of double boiler and add beeswax. Heat until completely melted and stir to combine thoroughly. Add a couple drops of essential oil if desired.
3. Pour salve into clean glass jars and store in a cool, dark place.

The smell of lavender will linger for hours.

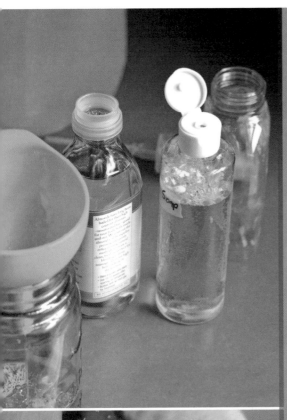

Basic Shampoo

- $^1/_4$ cup distilled water
- $^1/_4$ cup liquid castile soap
- $^1/_2$ teaspoon almond oil
- 1–2 drops lemongrass essential oil

1. Shake the ingredients until well combined in a foamer, which can be found at most department stores.
2. Apply a handful to your palm and gently massage into your scalp. Rinse and dry.

Rose Bath Salts

- 2 cups Epsom salts
- 8–10 drops rose essential oil
- $^1/_4$ cup rose petals, dried

1. Mix Epsom salts and essential oil until well combined. Add in rose petals and toss to evenly distribute.
2. Drop a couple tablespoons into a hot bath. The warm water will dissolve the salts into the bath and pull out additional hidden oils from the dried rose petals.

Beauty Mask

Honey from your own beehive can create pampering beauty products in addition to tasty treats. Work this soothing face mask into your beauty regimen.

- 3 tablespoons honey
- 2 tablespoons plain yogurt

1. Mix ingredients together in a small bowl.
2. Apply to face and let sit for ten minutes. Rinse off with warm water.

Conclusion
THE ROAD AHEAD

No matter how you grow, raise, and create, all homesteads are connected to the seasons. In summertime, the garden is exploding with produce, bees are buzzing, and the kitchen is humming with activity as the harvest gets preserved. Then, as the days get shorter, the homestead gets quieter.

It's a natural cycle that can feel very calming to be connected to once again, just like homesteaders before us. The bumpy ride of homesteading may have left you wiped out and ready to hole up inside for a couple months with some hot chocolate and a few good books. Or it may have left you with bigger and better plans you're itching to get started on. Regardless of how you approach the quiet months ahead, it's important to take stock of where you've come in a few short months.

Early homesteaders had a make-it or break-it deal. They had to survive for five years in order to own their land out West. Your goals for next season could be lofty or humble, but taking a look around can be both enlightening and empowering.

How did it go? Did you end up with enough jam for sandwiches all winter? Did you find a way to use all of those chicken or duck eggs? Did the kumquat tree in your living room produce fruit? Give yourself credit for any and all success, no matter how big or small.

Dust off that well-used garden journal and make some notes now, before winter turns the last few months into a distant memory. Note whether you want to try more beans next year or if you could have used sixty pounds of tomatoes to can instead of just thirty. Sketch down ideas of how you could better lay out the garden plot or ideas for an improved chicken coop. Want to put in additional window boxes? Expand your compost system? Do more research on a heritage livestock breed you are interested in raising next year?

Wintertime is nature's way of telling us we need a break. Hibernate inside and take it easy. Next year your homestead will grow a little bigger, so you better rest up while you can, for more prosperous days lie ahead.

References

Stake Your Claim

Boswell, Victor. United States Department of Agriculture. *Victory Gardens*. Government Printing Office, 1942.

Jones, Marvin. *How War Food Saved American Lives: Addresses and Statements*. National Capital Press, 1947.

Tucker, David. *Kitchen Gardening in America: A History*. Iowa State University Press, 1993.

United States Department of Agriculture. *Victory Garden: Leader's Handbook*. Government Printing Office, 1943.

Grow Your Own

American Community Garden Association, communitygarden.org.

Appelhof, Mary. *Worms Eat My Garbage: How to Set Up and Maintain a Worm Composting System*. Flower Press, 1997.

Elliot, Carl. *Maritime Northwest Garden Guide*. Tilth, 2000.

Hemenway, Toby. *Gaia's Garden: A Guide to Home-Scale Permaculture*. Chelsea Green, 2001.

Kingsolver, Barbara. *Animal, Vegetable, Miracle: A Year of Food Life*. Harper Perennial, 2008.

Mother Earth News. Ogden Publishing.

National Agricultural Library, nal.usda.gov.

Pollan, Michael. *Second Nature: A Gardener's Education*. Grove Press, 2003.

Seymour, John. *The Self-Sufficient Gardener*. Dolphin Books, 1979.

Trail, Gayla. You Grow Girl: The Lazy Gardener's Seed Starting Chart, yougrowgirl.com/2006/03/31/the-lazy-gardeners-seed-starting-chart.

USDA Plant Database, plants.usda.gov/plants.

Citified Critters
American Beekeeping Federation, abfnet.org.
American Dairy Goat Association, adga.org.
BackyardChickenForum, backyardchickens
.com/forum/index.php.
Flotum, Kim. *The Backyard Bee Keeper: An Absolute Beginner's Guide to Keeping Bees in Your Yard and Garden.* Quarry Books, 2009.
Holderread, David. *Storey's Guide to Raising Ducks: Breeds, Care, Health.* Storey Publishing, 2000.
Kilarski, Barbara. *Keep Chickens! Tending Small Flocks in Cities, Suburbs, and Other Small Spaces.* Storey Publishing, 2003.
Luttmann, Gail. *Raising Milk Goats Successfully.* Williamson Publishing Company, 1986.
McMurray Hatchery, mcmurrayhatchery.com/index.html.
PDXBackyardChix, groups.yahoo.com/group/PDXBackyardChix/?yguid=356423143.

Preserving the Harvest
Ball Blue Book of Preserving. Alltrista Consumer Products, 2004.
Chesman, Andrea. *Serving Up the Harvest: Celebrating the Goodness of Fresh Vegetables.* Storey Publishing, 2007.
Costenbader, Carol. *The Big Book of Preserving the Harvest.* Storey Publishing, 2002.
Environmental Working Group, ewg.org.
Farmers Market Coalition, farmersmarket coalition.org.
Findley, Mary, and Linda Formichelli. *The Complete Idiot's Guide to Green Cleaning, 2nd ed.* Penguin Publishing, 2009.
Hollender, Jeffery. *Naturally Clean: The Seventh Generation Guide to Safe & Healthy Non-Toxic Cleaning.* New Society Publishers, 2006.
Hupping, Carol. *Stocking Up: The Classic Preserving Guide.* Rodale Press, 1986.
Local Harvest, localharvest.org.
National Center for Home Food Preservation, uga.edu/nchfp.
Shephard, Susan. *Pickled, Potted, and Canned: How the Art and Science of Food Preserving Changed the World.* Simon & Schuster, 2000.
Skin Deep, Environmental Working Group, cosmeticsdatabase.com.
Slow Food USA, slowfoodusa.org.

Index